C000300777

THE ANOREXIC MIND

THE ANOREXIC MIND

Marilyn Lawrence

Routledge
Taylor & Francis Group

LONDON AND NEW YORK

First published 2008 by Karnac Books Ltd.

Published 2019 by Routledge
2 Park Square, Milton Park, Abingdon, Oxon OX14 4RN
52 Vanderbilt Avenue, New York, NY 10017, USA

Routledge is an imprint of the Taylor & Francis Group, an informa business

Copyright © 2008 by Marilyn Lawrence

The rights of Marilyn Lawrence to be identified as the author of this work have been asserted in accordance with §§ 77 and 78 of the Copyright Design and Patents Act 1988.

All rights reserved. No part of this book may be reprinted or reproduced or utilised in any form or by any electronic, mechanical, or other means, now known or hereafter invented, including photocopying and recording, or in any information storage or retrieval system, without permission in writing from the publishers.

Notice:
Product or corporate names may be trademarks or registered trademarks, and are used only for identification and explanation without intent to infringe.

British Library Cataloguing in Publication Data

A C.I.P. for this book is available from the British Library

ISBN: 9781855753839 (pbk)

Edited, designed, and produced by Communication Crafts

For Halo

CONTENTS

Margot Waddell

Since it was founded in 1920, the Tavistock Clinic has developed a wide range of developmental approaches to mental health which have been strongly influenced by the ideas of psychoanalysis. It has also adopted systemic family therapy as a theoretical model and a clinical approach to family problems. The Clinic is now the largest training institution in Britain for mental health, providing postgraduate and qualifying courses in social work, psychology, psychiatry, and child, adolescent, and adult psychotherapy, as well as in nursing and primary care. It trains about 1,700 students each year in over sixty courses.

The Clinic's philosophy aims at promoting therapeutic methods in mental health. Its work is based on the clinical expertise that is also the basis of its consultancy and research activities. The aim of this Series is to make available to the reading public the clinical, theoretical, and research work that is most influential at the Tavistock Clinic. The Series sets out new approaches in the understanding and treatment of psychological disturbances in children, adolescents, and adults, both as individuals and in families.

The Anorexic Mind is the culmination of thirty years of clinical practice, teaching, and consultation about the often intractable problems of anorexia and bulimia. One of the many strengths of the book is its dual focus: it moves between psychoanalytic work in the consulting room on the one hand, and work with very ill people in inpatient settings on the other. As a consequence, the respective chapters draw both on long-term intensive psychodynamic psychotherapy and also on approaches to mental health that stem from traditions that lie at the heart of the work of the Tavistock—namely, the importance, especially in high-risk illnesses like eating disorders, of multidisciplinary teamwork, and also the significance of the developmental perspective. This latter is rooted in the now widespread practice of infant observation among health care professionals of all kinds.

The book offers three sorts of historical perspective: the chronology of the manifestation and treatment of such illnesses, dating back to the early Christian anchorites; the history of psychoanalytic thought on the subject; and the history of early feeding patterns from infancy through childhood and adolescence—that is, the family history of the sufferers themselves. So, while acknowledging the fascinating and perplexing area of cultural and sociological determinants, the book predominantly focuses on the ardours, but also the rewards, of work with this patient population. The starting point is recent developments in the psychoanalytic understanding of the field. With utmost clarity and open-mindedness, the author lays out a picture of the available treatment models. Throughout, the central stress is on the close links between disordered eating and underlying disordered relationships, which the case discussions exemplify in moving, even searing, detail. This book will be of enormous value to all professionals working in so troubled a field, as well as to parents and patients alike.

ACKNOWLEDGEMENTS

Thanks to all my patients over the past thirty years. My thanks are due to all staff and students on the Tavistock MA course, Working with People with Eating Disorders, especially to Gianna Williams and Roberta Mondadori.

Thanks to Margot Waddell for her excellent editorial guidance, her patience, but also, on occasion, her very helpful impatience.

Thanks to Geoffrey Pearson for continual support and occasional inspiration.

I would like to acknowledge the kind permission of the *International Journal of Psychoanalysis* to reproduce previously published material in chapters 4 and 6.

ABOUT THE AUTHOR

Marilyn Lawrence is a Member of the British Psychoanalytical Society and a Fellow of the Institute of Psychoanalysis. She works in the Adult Department of the Tavistock Clinic and in private practice in London. She has a long-standing interest in eating disorders, as well as in gender and sexual development. Her published works include *The Anorexic Experience* (1984), *Fed Up and Hungry* (1989), and *Fighting Food* (1990). She is currently Programme Director of the Foundation Course in Psychoanalytic Psychotherapy at the Tavistock and Portman NHS Foundation Trust and is Director of Publications at the Institute of Psychoanalysis.

THE ANOREXIC MIND

CHAPTER ONE

Introduction

This book represents an attempt to understand the states of mind that underlie the serious eating disorders of anorexia and bulimia. Compulsive overeating or binge-eating is also considered, particularly as it relates to anorexia.

The ideas in the book have developed through two distinct areas of professional practice. The first is my own direct clinical work as a psychoanalyst, treating adult patients who suffer from eating disorders. The second is as a learning resource to the staff who run specialist units caring for patients with eating disorders. In recent years I have worked with colleagues on the MA programme at the Tavistock Clinic, Working with People with Eating Disorders, and am greatly indebted to both students and colleagues for what we have managed to learn together.

The perspective of the book is psychoanalytic inasmuch as it assumes that mental functioning is unconscious as well as conscious and that, as human beings, we only very partially understand our own motivation. However, the book is not written exclusively for psychoanalysts—quite the contrary. An approach that helps practitioners to find meaning in the illnesses of their patients is likely to be helpful to mental health workers from a range of different backgrounds. Following many years of working with psychiatrists, nurses, dieticians, and others concerned with the specialist care of eating-disorder patients, it seems clear that the most difficult task for the professionals is to go on thinking about their patients. This is a group of patients with many features in common, but perhaps chief among these is a real difficulty in thinking about themselves and their own psychological predicament. Staff, too, can become caught up in the mechanics of treatment, focusing on target weights, the body mass index (BMI), the rules and regulations that govern the unit, and the setting in which they work, while at the same time failing to understand in psychological terms what it might be that the patients are reacting to. Faced with the constant pressure and challenge from the patients to give up thinking, it should not surprise us that sometimes we do just that. A psychoanalytic framework can provide a structure that can enable thinking to be recovered, even if the work itself seems a long way from psychoanalysis as we normally understand it.

I also want to promote psychoanalysis and psychoanalytic psychotherapy as effective treatments for patients with eating disorders, though I fully acknowledge that this also has its difficulties. The psychoanalytic literature on eating disorders is developing well, and in spite of a current preoccupation with short, focused treatments, we have every reason to be optimistic that psychoanalysis is providing a model for treatment as well as a framework for understanding. The difficulties as well as the advantages of treating patients with a psychoanalytically based form of psychotherapy are fully discussed in chapter 3.

The fact that the book has this dual focus—psychoanalysis on the one hand, and work in inpatient settings on the other—gives it, I suspect, an uneven quality. I am aware that I move from one treatment setting to another and that very different kinds of work are being described. However, I believe and hope that this dual focus will be a strength of my approach. The unconscious processes that we can identify in the consulting room can and need to be recognized and addressed within the very ill patients in hospital.

Eating disorders became much more common in the second half of the twentieth century and continue to be prevalent, especially among young women. This has led some researchers, including myself, to speculate about the social origins of these conditions. While such speculation is interesting and it is potentially important to make links between psychiatry, psychoanalysis, and other branches of the human sciences, the stance taken here is that eating disorders are manifestations of mental illness. This statement, of course, begs the question of what is meant by "mental illness" and to what extent mental illness really parallels physical illness. These are questions I cannot answer, but however one understands it, I do regard young people who develop an eating disorder as being in serious trouble and needing help. Often the patients do not recognize themselves as ill. They sometimes claim to be making "lifestyle choices", and this kind of claim is supported by the proliferation of the so-called "pro-ana"—meaning pro-anorexia—websites, offering support and encouragement for the lifestyle choice of starvation. Worryingly, one sometimes reads articles by intelligent journalists who regard anorexics as in some way icons of our age. It is also noteworthy that the recent guidelines from the National Institute for Clinical Excellence (NICE) on the treatment of eating disorders do not mention that these are mental illnesses. I think this does imply a degree of collusion with the denial of the patients that they are in need of help. It is also particularly unhelpful and confusing for their parents, who can often react much more helpfully when they realize that their children have serious emotional difficulties underlying their behaviour. It seems to me essential that we keep the suffering of the anorexic and bulimic patients at the forefront of our thinking. I shall therefore examine the links and similarities between eating disorders and other forms of mental illness. Chapter 2 looks at the way eating disorders have manifested themselves and been understood historically, with special reference to psychiatric and psychoanalytic accounts.

The most common age of onset of eating disorders is adolescence, somewhere between 12 and 20. However, there are many reports in the literature of children as young as 8 years becoming anorexic. It is also possible for people to develop an eating disorder at any time later in life. Early in my career, I met a woman suffering from what seemed to be typical anorexia nervosa at age 70. The onset of the illness seemed to have been linked to the retirement of her husband and the huge change in lifestyle that this brought about. Sometimes illnesses that appear to be late-onset eating disorders are, in fact, second or subsequent episodes of illnesses that began much earlier in life. It is sometimes impossible to be certain, but I strongly suspect that the vast majority of eating disorders begin in adolescence, or earlier, and probably have their antecedents in infancy. It is perhaps not surprising that the eating disorder may recur as a seeming "solution" to developmental difficulties that occur later in life.

I therefore spend quite a lot of time in this book thinking about development, from infancy through childhood and adolescence, trying to capture and recreate a sense of what mental life might have been like, in the years before they became ill, for those individuals who end up as adult patients (chapters 3–6). This emphasis on development is not based on a quest for the causes of eating disorders. We do not know the causes of many illnesses, in particular mental illnesses, and I feel under no obligation to offer a theory about what causes eating disorders. I think the search for causes, which has tended to bedevil work in this area, has occurred partly because eating disorders appear to strike out of the blue. We are often told that some of these at least are the most promising young women of their generation, who "suddenly" develop serious mental illness. My interest in the infancy, childhood, and adolescence of the patients is rooted in my belief in the continuity of life and development in human individuals. Storms only appear to come "out of the blue" because when we look back, we don't know what to look for. We were looking for huge grey clouds when we should have been noting changes in humidity. We look for a hurricane when really it is the very stillness of the air which should have alerted us.

This emphasis on continuity should not be taken to mean that I do not believe in change. This whole book—but especially chapters 3, 7, and 8—is about how people can change in some very profound and fundamental ways. I am not referring here to changes in behaviour, but to changes that can take place in the minds of individuals, altering and enriching our sense of who we are and how we can feel related to other people.

I have tried to convey the balance that I feel between acknowledging the terrible seriousness of the underlying illness in some cases of eating disorders as against the hope of recovery. I particularly address this in chapter 6, where I try to understand more about the life-and-death struggle that I believe is taking place within the patients.

I shall be suggesting that eating disorders, like other forms of illness, vary in severity and also in the emotional availability of the patients for treatment. It is very important, before deciding on the best course of action, to make a careful assessment of each patient and to try to gauge the quality and depth of the problem. The majority of the cases require a degree of teamwork, involving psychotherapists working alongside GPs and local community teams—something to which many psychotherapists are unaccustomed. This is fully elaborated in chapter 7.

These patients, and the way they show us their difficulties, represent a huge challenge to us as mental health professionals, but also as human beings. There certainly are no simple answers, and perhaps in some cases there are no answers. The exploration of these difficulties takes us, I think, to the very heart of the human condition: our vulnerability and our need to depend on others: our parents firstly, and then the relationships that we are subsequently able to make.

CHAPTER TWO

Historical perspectives and contemporary debates

The manipulation of the size of the body by deliberately limiting food intake (or, indeed, by overeating) has probably been practised by certain sections of every civilized society. However, it is the tradition we call asceticism, often associated with religious fervour, that has become particularly associated with the eating disorders of anorexia and bulimia. Asceticism nearly always involves fasting, sometimes in extreme forms. Other forms of what we might now call "self-harm", such as self-flagellation and self-cutting, have often formed a part of both Eastern and Western religious traditions.

Well-known examples would include the early Christian anchorites and anchoresses who practised extreme forms of self-denial, living in caves as desert hermits. Underlying these practices is a dualistic understanding of mind/soul and body. The body is viewed, like the external world, as essentially sinful. The mind/soul can achieve perfection only if the body can be subdued and overcome. The body is felt to be an enemy of the soul, which it attempts to keep trapped in sinful imperfection (Lawrence, 1979). These beliefs have been explicit and dominant in the Christian tradition at certain points in history, such as the Gnostic heresy in the early church and in the Catharism of the medieval period. However, I believe that this dualistic thinking is actually very prevalent, and all of us to a greater or lesser extent experience our bodies as separate from our minds. Very often the body is regarded as inferior to the mind. The body is essentially uncontrollable. This is especially apparent in adolescence and again in the course of the ageing process. In patients with eating disorders, the uncontrollable nature of the body cannot be accepted. In fact of course, the mind is also uncontrollable. If we are able to think, we have no control over what thoughts come into our minds. These extreme religious practices, although ostensibly aimed at controlling and subduing the body, are in fact also a means of controlling the mind, which becomes utterly dominated by the body and its sufferings and quite unable to think. Paradoxically, although the anorexic and the aesthete both regard their body as the enemy, both are able to think of little else. Another problem with the body is its mortality, whereas the soul is widely believed to live for ever. As we shall see, anorexic patients find the idea of death unacceptable and believe they are indeed immortal.

Rudolph Bell (1985) writes about a series of religious figures, the female Italian saints from the thirteenth century onwards. He provides some fascinating snapshots of their ascetic practices and tries to make links between these medieval religious divas and the anorexic girls of the modern era. He is undoubtedly correct that young women like Catherine of Siena, who starved, cut, and beat herself over many years, would today be regarded as highly disturbed. He is also correct when he indicates that these women eventually lost control of their ascetic practices and became unable to eat, just like the contemporary anorexic does. But is it really helpful or relevant to consider these ancient and medieval religious women as being in some way the same as contemporary anorexics as Bell does, when he labels the whole ascetic movement of the medieval period, "Holy Anorexia"? Where I think the medieval saints differ from the contemporary anorexics is in the consciousness of their motivation. One of the most significant features of modern-day anorexia is that while the patients are clearly highly motivated to pursue their relentless goal of absolute thinness, they do not seem to know what it is that motivates them. They often come up with the idea that they are "too fat", a statement that seems delusional to the observer but might relate to some very uncomfortable internal states of mind. The medieval saints and the desert mothers, on the other hand, were quite clear and explicit that they were trying to free their souls or their minds from the prison of the body, perceived as sinful. They were aiming for spiritual perfection. Now, it may be that some contemporary anorexics do in fact have a similar motivation, but if they do, it is unspoken and, I imagine, largely unconscious. What strikes us forcefully about the anorexics of today is that while they know they have to lose more and more weight, they don't actually know why. But I am not quite certain here. One exception would seem to be the celebrated case of Ellen West (Binswanger, 1944), where, as I shall indicate, the patient did seem to have something of the same or parallel motivation as her saintly forebears, although she expressed it in terms more apt for the age in which she lived.

In a medieval world, where views about the dualistic nature of humankind were largely shared, the ascetic practices of the saints certainly seemed extreme, but they did not seem necessarily mad. In fact, the women were often questioned about their motivation by the priests and bishops, who asked whether they were certain they were not being mislead (by the devil), but the discourse stayed firmly within religious parameters.

Self-starvation (and other eating disorders) first became identified and categorized as forms of mental illness in the closing decades of the nineteenth century. In the 1870s Gull in London and Lasegue in France published papers describing the syndrome of Anorexia Nervosa (Gull, 1873) or Anorexie Mentale (Lasegue, 1874). Freud was at medical school at this time, and it is clear from a number of references in his work that he was quite familiar with this disorder.

This was an age when much important psychiatric observation was taking place, and a number of psychiatric illnesses were identified and recorded for the first time.

The descriptions that Gull and Lasegue record are detailed and astute. Lasegue describes eight patients aged between 18 and 32. He interestingly emphasizes the emotional origins of the illness, writing of "A young girl . . . [who] suffers from some emotion which she avows or conceals. Generally it relates to some real or imaginary project, to a violence done to some sympathy, or to some more or less conscient desire."

Gull was more concerned with a description of the signs and symptoms. His prescription for treatment of the condition was simple: "The treatment required is obviously that which is fitted for persons of unsound mind. The patients should be fed at regular intervals, and surrounded by persons who would have moral control over them; relations and friends being generally the worst attendants."

It is of interest to note that neither Gull nor Lasegue attempted to incorporate anorexia into any other known illness or syndrome. Although they clearly wondered about its links with hysterical illness, neither tried to describe it as a "special case" of hysteria. Although some attempts have been made to link anorexia to other psychiatric syndromes, and to distinguish between different forms of anorexia on the basis of its resemblance to other conditions (e.g. hysterical and obsessional anorexia, see Dally, Gomez, & Isaacs, 1979, for example), contemporary psychiatry has tended to follow Gull and Lasegue in making eating disorders a distinct syndrome in themselves, not explicitly related to other illnesses. In a contemporary textbook on the history of psychiatry (Berrios & Porter, 1995), eating disorders occupy a special section, with no sense of their link with other psychological states. This would seem to be an accurate reflection of current psychiatric thinking, but, as I shall go on to suggest, this may not have helped us to understand the differences within the category "eating disorder" or to accurately plot the links with psychotic illness, personality disorder, and borderline states. It might also have impeded our progress in thinking about the relationship between anorexia and other developmental disorders, such as autism.

In his account of the infantile neurosis of the Wolf Man, Freud mentions the well-known neurosis that occurs in girls at puberty, in which aversion to sexuality expresses itself in aversion to food, or anorexia (Freud, 1918b [1914], p. 106).

This is a throw-away comment, but nonetheless an intriguing one. Freud's linking of anorexia with both adolescence and an aversion to sex set out a line of thinking that has dominated the debate ever since. Today in British psychiatry, the most commonly used expositionary model, the "regression hypothesis" (Crisp, 1986), is based upon just such a dual link.

A further very interesting and valuable aspect of Freud's comment is that it occurs within the context of discussion of the "normal" neuroses of childhood, which include periods of appetite disturbance. This line of thinking was taken up by Anna Freud (1958) and, as we shall see, by later object-relations psychoanalysts, most notably Melanie Klein.

The early psychoanalysts continued to show an interest in eating and its disorders. Karl Abraham writing in 1916, was one of the earliest psychoanalysts to take an interest in eating as such, and to link it fully with the development of object relations. He writes of a cannibalistic phase of development in which the prevailing phantasy is of oral incorporation of the object. In "The First Pregenital Stage of the Libido", Abraham discusses the case of a young simple schizophrenic man completely preoccupied by sucking and drinking milk. This patient described his "cannibalistic ideas" (quotation marks are Abraham's) saying that as a child he had the idea that loving someone was exactly the same as the idea of eating something good.

Abraham goes on to describe a woman patient in analysis who was severely troubled by compulsive overeating. Each night she would wake up several times with a voracious hunger, which she would proceed to satisfy with large meals (Abraham, 1916). He gives this case as an example of an instinct denied satisfaction which regressively manifests itself at an earlier (oral) level of development. He tells us that she was very determined not to give up her nightly satisfactions. It is interesting, though not perhaps surprising, that psychoanalysis should from early on take an interest in such a symptom. It has taken psychiatry many more years to recognize compulsive overeating as a symptom worthy of treatment, and then only because of one of its most obvious effects: obesity.

Fenichel, in his textbook of 1943, helpfully discusses the possible relationship of anorexia nervosa to other kinds of pathology. He suggests that in some cases it may be a simple hysterical symptom, or a symptom related to an obsessional or depressive illness. In others it will be the tip of a much more insidious iceberg, in which the whole personality, and its relation to others and to reality, is grossly disturbed and distorted. This is what we would recognize today as the core of the Anorexia Nervosa syndrome. He mentions a patient who, he says, has not gone beyond an extremely archaic stage of ego development, with the mother remaining the most important part of the patient's ego (p. 177). Again, most of us would very much agree with his formulations. In what follows, it is important to remember this distinction between eating disorders of different origins and different degrees of seriousness. In the most serious of the situations described by Fenichel, the patient has much more than a simple eating disorder. Rather, it is a pervasive developmental disorder in which all aspects of the personality are locked in a deadly conflict with the patient's own life.

"The Case of Ellen West"

Unsurprisingly, the analysts with the most contribution to make to the study and treatment of eating disorders have been those with strong links to inpatient settings.

In 1944 Ludwig Binswanger published his remarkable study, "The Case of Ellen West". She was treated as an inpatient by him in 1921. Binswanger, who identified himself as an existential psychoanalyst, first encountered Ellen West when she was already what we would term a chronic anorexic. She was admitted to Kreuzlingen Sanatorium with her husband at the age of 33, having been disturbed since her teenage years and seriously anorexic since age 20. The remarkable thing about the case of Ellen West is not the uniqueness of her story—it is all too familiar—but the capacity of the patient to talk and write about her experience and the capacity of her doctor to listen. Ellen West describes a lifelong dread of "ordinary" life. The physical facts of existence, the necessity of having a body, of being made of the corporeal stuff of life, appals her. She cannot bear it. She tries to satisfy herself with being brilliant, with doing "good works" aimed towards social change. But nothing satisfies her. Her only salvation, she finds, lies in the destruction of her physical body itself. This, she feels, will set her free. By the time she comes to Binswanger, she is habitually addicted to large doses of laxatives and weighs no more than 90 pounds.

In Binswanger's account, which is richly illustrated by the patient's own verbal and written material, we encounter for the first time the central dilemma for the anorexic. Everything that the external world sees as life-promoting—food, love, sex, procreation—seems to her to herald the death of her authentic self. Freedom seems to her to equal etherealness, lightness, non-existence.

Binswanger makes it clear that Ellen West has a problem with reality. She longs to be "an ethereal type", which to her is blond and slightly built, like the student she falls in love with and with whom she is obsessed for several years. In fact, she is a dark and well-built woman. Just like the anorexic patients of today, Ellen West cannot bear the reality of being limited by her physical body, which will age and ultimately die.

After a prolonged stay at Kreuzlingen, during which she continued to make numerous attempts at self-harm, Ellen West and her husband are given a choice. She can either stay, but with increased levels of monitoring and security, or she can go home and try to sort her life out with her husband. They choose the latter. She returns home, for the first time happy and contented. She eats without inhibition for the first time in many years before taking a fatal dose of poison, three days after her discharge.

Such a story—in which the chronic patient, after years of what feels like subjection to such compulsions, finally takes matters into her own hands—is probably not as unusual as we might think. What is unusual is the careful and respectful way it is documented and discussed.

Later developments

Helmut Thomä, another psychoanalyst working in a mental hospital setting, produced an astonishing series of thirty patients treated with psychoanalytic psychotherapy between 1950 and 1959 at Heidelberg University Psychiatric Hospital. His book *Anorexia Nervosa*, translated and published in English in 1967, is a treasure trove of case histories and detailed accounts of psychoanalytic psychotherapy with severely ill anorexic patients. His patients were treated five times weekly while in hospital and three to five times weekly on discharge.

The book describes the very encouraging results of this clinical trial—much better results, Thomä points out, than those from the Maudsley Hospital trial (Kay, 1953), where patients were treated with insulin, electro-shock, and sometimes leucotomy. In the Maudsley study, psychotherapy was found to be ineffective. Thomä concludes that this "presumably is due to some misapplication of psychoanalytic technique or theory" (Thomä, 1967, p. 64). He also comments on the high rates of attempted suicide among the Maudsley group. He says: "We must at least wonder whether the remarkable frequency of attempted suicide among these patients at the Maudsley Hospital was not due to the way in which diet control was enforced" (p. 65). Forty years on, such controversies concerning the most helpful ways to conduct inpatient treatment continue to rage.

Developments in psychoanalysis

A line of thinking opened up by Freud, and continued in the British tradition of Melanie Klein and some of her followers, has allowed some more fruitful thinking on eating disorders to develop. It is a line of thinking that has been particularly helpful in enabling us to think about infant development and has emphasized the continuities between the infant, the child, the adolescent, and the adult. Sometimes called the theories of Object Relations, this way of conceptualizing mental development emphasizes the pattern of relationships, unique to each individual, that is set up in infancy and continues in different forms through life. (The term "object" used in this way refers to people, in the sense that the "subject"—the individual under discussion—relates to others or objects. It is a useful shorthand used in contemporary psychoanalysis.) These early relationships and the figures that, in our minds, we relate to, are taken into our minds and become an important part of our selves. They influence our outlook, the way we think about ourselves, our unspoken and unthought assumptions. Such figures can be more, or less, benign and helpful to us. Given that the earliest of our relationships—that with the mother at the breast—is a feeding relationship, we would expect attitudes to food and eating, and any difficulties in this respect, to deeply reflect this early relational situation.

Melanie Klein wrote of the primal processes of introjection (taking in) and projection (expelling). For her, introjection, operative from the beginning of life, allows the primitive psyche to take in good things from the environment—initially food, but encompassing the love, care, and beauty of the mother, which are actually inseparable from the feeding process. It is repeated good experiences of this sort that lead to the instatement in the mind of a good internal figure, who can help and support the individual, particularly during periods of separation. The parallel process of projection allows the baby to rid itself of painful, unwanted feelings, which would otherwise threaten to overwhelm it. Of course, the environment of any infant will confront it with mixed experiences. No relationship is perfect. The infant needs to be able to preserve and nurture the good aspects of its relationships while at the same time being able to get rid of those unpleasant experiences that provoke its fury and hatred. One of the great strengths of Klein's writing is her acknowledgement of the role of phantasy in development and her understanding of how phantasy can interact with reality to support and facilitate development. (Following Klein, I am using the "ph" spelling, rather than "f", for phantasy. The usual convention is to use the "f" spelling if what is being referred to is conscious and "ph" if it is largely unconscious.)

One example of this is the near-universal phenomenon known as "wind". Mothers tend to be encouraged after a feed to help the baby to bring up its "wind". The crying baby is often felt to have "wind", something unpleasant in the stomach which interferes with the digestion and metabolizing of the good and nourishing milk and the good experience of having been fed. As well as the "good" milk, it seems as though something not-so-good has been taken in as well. Of course, there really is a phenomenon of taking in air as well as milk in a physical sense; however, in a parallel way, bad feelings—feelings of frustration, for example—might be taken in with the milk and in phantasy be expelled with the wind, allowing the baby to feel as though the good milk/mother has been preserved and sleep is possible.

Klein movingly describes the strength and power of the feelings and phantasies to which the infant is subject at these times. Again, emotions and physical sensations and processes become inseparable. The baby's hatred and frustration can be expressed through its wetting and messing, which in phantasy can be used to burn and poison the mother and her breast.

These psychological processes, so closely mirroring physical ones, are a normal and necessary aspect of human development—indeed, they could be regarded as the building blocks of emotional growth. Klein emphasizes the importance of balance in the development of personality. If projective processes become excessive, there is a danger that the infant will in phantasy force more and more unwanted aspects of itself into its object. The mother then comes to contain all the aggression and resentment in the mind of the infant, while the infant itself feels empty and impoverished.

Difficulties in the early mother–infant relationship can lead to difficulties in the feeding process. Practically all babies go through periods of feeding difficulty, perhaps seeming inhibited in feeding or uninterested in food. Alternatively, some babies may sometimes seem to feed in a greedy or aggressive way, seeming to wish to attack or devour the breast in a hateful way rather than sucking it in a loving way. Such difficulties are often associated with developmental milestones such as the introduction of solid food, short separations from the mother, the recognition of the role of the father, weaning. All of these produce difficulties in the relationship between infant and mother, which are then reflected in a feeding difficulty. In general, the feeding difficulties resolve as the relationship difficulties resolve and development continues. Occasionally feeding difficulties become entrenched, implying that some difficulty in the relationship has become stuck.

I am not here meaning to imply that all adolescents who go on to develop eating disorders have experienced serious feeding difficulties as infants. I am using the psychoanalytic descriptions of the writers associated with Melanie Klein to emphasize that from the beginning of life, eating—the taking in of food—is closely associated with the taking in of love and the primary relationship offered by the mother. This leads me to suppose that all feeding difficulties and eating disorders are associated with relationship difficulties: specifically, that there is a difficulty in feeling open and receptive to the good things that relationships with others might have to offer.

In fact—and this really comes as no surprise—many people who later develop eating disorders actually have experienced serious feeding difficulties as infants. There are no reliable statistics as far as I know, and some clinicians would not necessarily think to enquire about this. In my experience, when a careful history is taken, and the parents as well as the patient are consulted, it often emerges that there were quite serious feeding difficulties at an early stage in infancy. This suggests that the relationship difficulties that underlie the later manifestations of eating disorders in adolescents and young adults were present, if not easily discernable, in infancy.

One of the most helpful sources of knowledge and understanding about the events of early infancy and their significance is the practice of infant observation. This technique, based on psychoanalytic principles, involves the observation of a baby and its mother, on a weekly basis, for the first year or two of its life. This innovative method of learning about infant development—and much else besides—was pioneered at the Tavistock Clinic in the 1940s. It is now a requirement for all higher-level trainings in child, adolescent, and adult psychotherapy and is undertaken by many healthcare professionals, including some paediatric nurses and health visitors. There are a number of very informative papers that focus on feeding and feeding difficulties, based on observations of mothers and infants.

Sheila Miller (1998), for example, writes of an observation of an infant who failed to thrive initially but subsequently recovered. During the course of the observation, the feeding difficulty recurred, and again he recovered. This was linked to a rather subtle hostility on the part of the mother, although this showed itself more overtly later in the observation, when she allowed the baby to be bitten by a family pet.

Ellie Roberts (1998) writes about introjective processes in early infancy based on the observation of the feeding of several infants. These are fascinating snapshots of the development of these individual infants and their parents. We cannot generalize from these unique intimate relationships, but such examples do reinforce our view that difficulties in the process of taking in food are reflections of the difficulties in taking the parents into the mind as good and helpful objects.

It seems important to make the point here that I am not talking about "bad parents"—whatever we might mean by that. Life would be much simpler than it actually is if parents who love their children and do their very best to look after them could be sure that this was sufficient to ensure a smooth developmental path. The truth is that we often do not know why things go wrong in family relationships. Difficulties can be subtle and are almost always unintentional. And parents are only one factor in the equation. No two children are alike, and, as parents with more than one child all know, the same sort of approach has radically different effects on two siblings. There is no question in my mind that some children are very much more difficult to care for emotionally than are others.

Another very helpful line of thinking that has been opened up in recent years concerns the effects upon the mind of failures to negotiate and work through the Oedipus situation. It is the work of Ronald Britton (1989) and others that has led us to the realization that a failure to establish two parents firmly in the mind leads to severe mental limitation and sometimes ultimately to mental breakdown. It is this developmental difficulty that leads to the inability to think symbolically, a problem found in all eating-disorder patients as well as in other patients with serious difficulties. Dana Birksted-Breen (1989) has written about this problem in the analysis of an anorexic patient, in which the patient's longing for and terror of fusion with a maternal figure is vividly evident in the transference. These recent developments in psychoanalytic understanding are the starting point of the book.

As well as finding contemporary developments in psychoanalysis helpful, I have also been led back to Freud's earlier formulations concerning the dual nature of the instincts or drives. Writing in 1937 of the problems of masochism, a sense of guilt and the negative therapeutic reaction, he says,

> These phenomena are unmistakable indications of the presence of a power in mental life which we call the instinct of aggression or destruction according to its aims, and which we

trace back to the original death instinct of living matter. Only by the concurrent or mutually opposing action of the two primal instincts—Eros and the death instinct—never by one or the other alone, can we explain the rich multiplicity of the phenomena of life. [1937c, p. 243]

In the course of my work with the very seriously ill patients, I have found it impossible to disagree with him.

Eating disorders and dieting

When the media first began to take an interest in anorexia in the 1970s, it was often referred to as "the slimmer's disease". Journalists were quick to link the increase in numbers of anorexic girls with the marked preference for slim models and actresses and the promotion of slimming foods and diet plans.

While it is almost certainly no coincidence that anorexia flourishes in a culture where thinness is prized, dieting in itself does not cause anorexia. The overwhelming majority of people who diet to lose weight do so more or less successfully, but they do not become ill with an eating disorder. Having said that, many young people who go on to develop an eating disorder (though not all) begin by deliberate dieting to lose weight. So while dieting in itself does not lead to an eating disorder, it does appear to act as a trigger in certain individuals. It is certainly the case that in societies and cultures where food is in short supply, eating disorders are either unknown or very rare.

There is no doubt that young women working or training in fields that might emphasize the importance of a thin body (such as modelling, dancing, athletics) are in the highest-risk groups for eating disorders. But again, the vast majority of dancers and sportswomen do not have an eating disorder, although they will all be under constant pressure to control their weight very precisely.

When writers link the increasing prevalence of eating disorders with a social obsession with thinness, it often seems to be overlooked that, in fact, the opposite is true. We may be part of a Western culture that overvalues thinness, but the underlying trend in our societies is towards not thinness, but obesity. As well as soaring levels of obesity in all populations, including children, the average sizes of the ordinary population have increased very markedly in the last fifty years. The tendency to regard thinness as "special" may well be linked with these changes

So why does dieting and a preoccupation with weight and body shape push some people and not others into an eating disorder? Underlying all eating disorders are relationship disorders, and I think it is probably true to say that people who go on to develop the symptoms of an eating disorder already have the emotional relationship disorder that underlies it. One of the curious features of eating disorders is that sometimes the relationship disorder is not evident to family and friends prior to the onset of the symptoms with food, though with hindsight it can usually be recognized. The precise nature of this relationship disorder is something that I shall be trying to grasp and to which we will return many times in the course of this book.

Recently there has been speculation about the role of the very thin supermodels in promoting the "cult" of thinness and in making girls dissatisfied with their normal bodies. Some fashion houses have refused to employ models who are seriously underweight, and this has been applauded by some people concerned with the mental health of young people. I am not sure, however, that insisting that models weigh a few more pounds is really going to help very much.

It seems to me that what has become fashionable currently, and from time to time throughout recent history, is a deathly look. It is not just that girls who model expensive clothes are very thin, it is that they actively cultivate a look that has associations with death. The make-up is ghostly, and they appear cut off and out of touch with those watching them. They walk as if in some kind of fugue state, with no hint of interest in what is going on around them. All eyes are devouring them. They want and lack nothing. They are asexual, looking as though sexuality is beneath them. This, I think, is what appeals to certain impressionable young people. However thin the models were, if they giggled and flirted with the photographers, the whole situation would be entirely different. In chapter 7, I discuss in more detail this preoccupation with and idealization of death.

Overeating and obesity

Obesity is often written about as though it were in itself an eating disorder. In fact, of course, it is a physical condition of being over-weight, currently defined as a BMI of 30 or over. There are many reasons for individuals to become and to remain overweight, the most common of which is poor diet associated with poverty. In the developed world, foods high in fat and sugar are cheap foods. Eating healthily takes a certain amount of resolve when there is so much opportunity to do the opposite.

This is written at a time when, in the developed world, obesity is viewed as a very important health risk. Here in the UK we read daily of the lowered life expectancy and the many serious illnesses that are being associated with being overweight. Almost as often we read of government initiatives aimed at tackling the "crisis", particularly among children and young people.

In some individuals, overweight and obesity are associated not just with eating fattening foods, but with eating far too much of all sorts of foods. These people who habitually overeat may be considered to have an eating disorder.

There are many different ways to think about the unconscious motivations that may be involved. Certainly some individuals would appear to deal with a sense of loneliness, or perhaps psychic emptiness, by filling themselves up with food, much as the bulimic patient might do, or the anorexic long to do and frantically defend herself against doing. In this sense one could say that the person who overeats is responding like the anorexic and bulimic, in a physical way, to something that properly belongs in the realm of the mind and the emotions. On the other hand, she is respond-ing in a much more straightforward way: she feels empty, so she fills herself up. So there is a sense in which the person who over-eats is likely to be less ill, psychologically, than the person who develops inhibitions and defences against her impulses.

However, there is another aspect to overweight and obesity that I would like to explore. In our culture, and particularly among the young, to be fat is regarded as the worst possible condition. It is associated with greed, with ugliness, with stupidity. And yet quite a lot of young women *are* fat and seem very resistant to being thinner. In fact, most health professionals would agree that trying to help overweight people to become thin is extremely difficult. There is certainly no shortage of advice available on how to lose weight, and there are specialist services. And yet, quite a number of people resolutely stick with being part of a group that one can only call despised.

It seems to me that to understand this phenomenon one has to understand that for some people, shame or humiliation is part of their self-image. I am thinking specifically of women at the moment, particularly young women, as I think the meaning of being overweight is probably different for women and men, and at different stages in life.

A girl who is overweight as a child will, by the time she reaches puberty, already have become accustomed to a good deal of contempt and ridicule from her peers. Puberty itself does her no favours, often occurring earlier for her than for others and giving her a much more mature-looking body than she is ready for. Her physical maturation attracts attention, but not usually admiring attention. She may very well develop a tough shell to her character, a seeming indifference to snide remarks, criticisms, or—even worse—jokes about her size and shape, but underneath it she feels deeply ashamed of herself.

The question one always hears is, why don't overweight girls diet and lose weight? My hypothesis is that by the time they reach maturity, they have already grown accustomed to being noticed but not admired, and this is a familiar situation which they perpetuate.

> Mrs J was an obese woman in her early 30s. She liked to think of herself as a tough, strong person, though in fact she lived her life terrified of rejection. One of her earliest memories was of being at a family party and lifting up her skirt and showing her bottom, to the great hilarity of the company. It seems that at this early age she had learned to get attention by making a joke of her femininity, rather than being admired as a beautiful girl.

It is interesting to speculate on the relationship between anorexia and the experience of the obese girl. In the case of some (though not all) anorexics, I think it is this denigration of femininity, this shamed woman, that she so dreads. So for some anorexics, one of the driving forces of their illness is the avoidance of the very situation that the obese girl embraces. A significant minority of girls who become anorexic do have a history of having been overweight and may have glimpsed in themselves and in the gaze of others this image of ruined and degraded femininity.

Unlike the anorexics, overweight young women are likely to act out sexually, often having casual sexual relationships, which they pretend to enjoy but which actually wound them deeply and intensify their sense of shame. In the course of the chapters that follow, I shall from time to time mention similarities and differences in the psychopathology underlying anorexia, bulimia, and overeating.

I have attempted in this brief survey to mention some of the important historical developments in psychiatric and psychoanalytic thinking about eating disorders. I have also clearly indicated how my own thinking has been shaped in recent years both by the classical and the post-Kleinian traditions of psychoanalysis. Finally, I have tried to situate the book in the context of contemporary attitudes and concerns.

CHAPTER THREE

Psychotherapy

O nce they become established, eating disorders are notoriously difficult to treat. There is no single form of treatment that we can say categorically is effective in all or even most cases. The kind of treatment I discuss here is a form of psychotherapy, based on psychoanalytic principles, that I have found to be helpful to very many patients. The reasons I think that it is often helpful are twofold. The first is that this form of treatment seeks to understand the uniqueness of the individual. While I try to outline in succeeding chapters where the developmental difficulties may lie, each patient is different, and someone needs to take the time and effort to understand precisely what has gone wrong for this individual. This is what psychoanalytic psychotherapy aims to do. The second reason for the usefulness of this treatment lies in the fact that it is based on a relationship. In eating disorders, many relationships will have broken down and the patient will be more or less terrified of getting close to anyone. And yet this is precisely what she needs to do if she is to understand what has happened to her and begin to find a way forward in her development.

Making a helpful relationship with a patient with an eating disorder is a complex process, as I hope I shall demonstrate. Although it may be painfully evident to us that the patient desperately needs help, in her mind she is completely self-sufficient. This is a state of mind that Janine Chasseguet-Smirgel (2005) has termed "autarkic", referring to a political system that emphasizes self-sufficiency and is highly restrictive in terms of its contact with its neighbours. As I have noted in the chapter on assessment (chapter 8), some patients are very much more difficult to make contact with than others, and in the most serious cases the patient shows little interest in anyone else at all. I find it quite understandable that some mental health professionals have looked for solutions that do not require the patients to make relationships. A popular suggestion currently is that the patients should be encouraged to undertake internet-based self-help programmes, following the principles of cognitive behaviour therapy. While such programmes might in themselves be thoughtfully constructed and very helpful to some people, the situation that results in anorexia seems to be one in which only self-help is permissible. The developmental impasse seems to be centred on the utter dread of allowing anyone to help, of feeling that ordinary human dependency is to do with "weakness", that needing to turn to someone means becoming an abject wretch whom everyone will despise. Psychoanalytic psychotherapy and all the many interventions based on psychoanalysis fundamentally challenge that position. While it is possible to recover from an eating disorder without psychoanalysis or psychoanalytic psychotherapy, I do not think it is possible to recover without finding a relationship on which to depend.

Issues of technique

It is sometimes said that patients with an eating disorder, who by definition have a serious difficulty with dependent relationships, will be unable to use the ordinary techniques derived from psychoanalysis. These include the technique of free association, whereby the patient is asked to try to say whatever comes into her mind. This means that the interaction is not determined by the therapist, who listens and not only responds to the surface of the material presented but attempts also to understand underlying anxieties and concerns, especially those connected with the relationship with the therapist as it unfolds. I must say, I find the undetermined nature of the psychotherapy setting particularly helpful and important. The patients are very often lonely and deeply unhappy, and they need to be able to show the therapist their difficulties in their own way. Of course, it does mean that the therapist has to be sensitive to the nonverbal as well as the verbal communications and aspects of the relationship, but this is true with any patient, not just an anorexic or bulimic patient.

It has sometimes been suggested that patients with an eating disorder cannot manage intensive treatment and should therefore only be offered once-weekly treatment. In my experience this is simply not true. Patients who are very vulnerable and disturbed often benefit greatly from very frequent contact. They may not always be able to use their sessions in a very ordinary way, but this is no reason for depriving them of the contact they so much need. It may be challenging for the therapist to have to sit with a very silent patient, for example, but it is certainly not impossible. I would therefore suggest that the patient should be offered treatment as frequently as can be managed. I can think of a number of child and adolescent psychotherapists at the Tavistock who have very successfully treated anorexic or bulimic adolescents in three-times-weekly psychotherapy and who have probably helped the patient to avoid a hospital admission.

I discuss in chapter 6 the way in which anorexic patients in particular appear to fear being intruded upon in much the same way as patients who have been abused. I suggest that this fear of intrusion is linked with a very intrusive object in the mind of the patient. I further suggest that this intrusive object is linked with the patient's own intrusiveness, particularly with regard to the relationship between the parents. The existence of this intrusive object has very important and far-reaching implications for the treatment of the patients.

In my view, it is absolutely impossible for the therapist to avoid feeling, and being perceived as, intrusive. This is not a particularly comfortable position for the therapist to find him/herself in, and it can be particularly difficult if the therapist him/herself has a need to be seen as "good" or skilful. Of course we all like to have a feeling of doing our work well, but, with eating-disorder patients, doing our work well often necessarily entails feeling clumsy and foolish and utterly unwanted.

In reality it is a complex situation. The patient consciously feels that she wants to be self-sufficient and that she can be self-sufficient. She absolutely doesn't want and doesn't need any of the kind of mental food in the way of understanding that we might be able to offer. Underneath that, however, the patient is desperate for contact, extremely dependent and infantile, longing for fusion with an idealized object. How is one to address this complexity? Essentially, the only way we can: by commenting on and interpreting the immediate situation in the consulting room, while at the same time keeping in mind the unconscious anxieties that underlie it. So while I might say that the patient seems as though she is frightened of me, as though I am going to force my words into her, I will be thinking, but not saying, how greedy she is afraid she is for every single word I will ever utter.

This, I think, is why intensive treatment is so useful. If the patient allows us any emotional contact with her at all, it is likely to stir up a deep and terrifying longing for our total care. This will be much easier for the patient to bear if she has a session tomorrow, even if it is a session in which she feels she has to keep silent. This is an important issue for psychotherapy organizations like the Tavistock Clinic, who offer assessments to patients but then have a waiting-list for treatment. A good assessment of possibly several sessions is likely to result in some emotional contact being made with the patient, often contact of quite an intense kind. If the patient then feels "dropped" during a wait for a treatment vacancy, the consequences can be serious. I have known of a number of cases where serious worsening of symptoms or acting out of other kinds has followed a successful assessment but where treatment did not very swiftly follow. Anorexic patients are not so much terrified of being offered five sessions a week as terrified of being offered *only* five sessions a week.

I think the traditional stance of the psychoanalytic practitioner is vital and is very much appreciated by the patients. However much they may experience us as intrusive, we will not, in reality, intrude into their lives. We have clear time boundaries, and there can be no doubts about our professional role. We have a code of ethics that supports us in this. Much as patients may sometimes complain about us being unfriendly, it is actually a huge relief that we know the limits, to prevent the patients from intruding (too much) into our lives as well as us into theirs. Our neutrality is also very helpful. One of the aims of treatment is to enable the patients to achieve and to stay in a state of conflict about their own development, rather than taking the option of shutting it down. They need a therapist who can comment to them from neutral ground about it all, not someone who is going to take sides.

Conditions and limitations

Having outlined the case for intensive psychoanalytic treatment, there are of course drawbacks and reservations. One of these is the need to pay attention to the physical health of the patient. The analytic setting does not allow us to act as nurse or physician to the patient, and it is sometimes argued that psychotherapy is unsafe as it cannot provide its own medical backup. In reality, I have rarely found difficulty in securing the cooperation of medical or psychiatric colleagues; on the contrary, I have often found a degree of collaboration on these difficult patients very valuable.

A second reservation would be the need for a good assessment. As I make clear in the chapter on life and death issues (chapter 7), there are patients suffering from anorexia and bulimia who have very little capacity for development. There is always a danger that a patient is, in fact, looking for a witness to their self-destructiveness rather than a chance to rejoin life. The seriousness of the patient's physical condition does not always reflect the extent of the deadliness of the patient's state of mind. Chronic patients sometimes maintain themselves at low weights, but weights consistent with life. But their lives may be lived in a quite deadly and hateful way, narrow and constricted, full of grievance and resentment. They sometimes seek a consultation at a particular point in their lives when they cannot fail to notice the passage of time, but may be completely unwilling to allow their psychic equilibrium to be upset by the threat of change.

In order for outpatient psychotherapy to be a realistic option, I do think patient and therapist need to share approximately the same reality about the patient's situation. While they might not agree about exactly what is wrong, or indeed might not know what is wrong, I think there has to be agreement that something is wrong. I do not think it is possible to sustain a therapeutic alliance with an anorexic or bulimic patient who insists that nothing is wrong.

Finally, there is a real risk of acting out. The danger is that the patient, under the sway of negative feelings towards the therapist, will act self-destructively, either by staying away or by actively losing weight or some other form of self-harm. If she can come to a session and be silent, bringing her anorexia into the session, the work can slowly proceed.

Competition between differing treatment methods and models

Although I am here putting forward the method of treatment with which I am most familiar and which I know to be effective, I am not wanting to disparage other forms of therapy that can also be helpful. There is no one form of treatment that we can be sure works, and we must stay open-minded and, above all, think about what kind of treatment may suit any particular individual patient at a particular point in her illness.

Family work and family therapy

Given the difficulties these patients have in their minds in effecting a psychic separation from their families, the question has been raised as to the possibility of work with the existing family. Much good work has been undertaken with the families of anorexic and bulimic patients (e.g. Minuchin, Rosman, & Baker, 1978; Selvini-Palazzoli, 1974). The early family-therapy pioneers mostly assumed that the family was in some way responsible for either the origins or maintenance of the symptoms, an assumption that has created many tensions over the decades between the families of the patients and the professionals who treat them.

A series of studies took place at the Maudsley Hospital into the efficacy of family therapy (Eisler, Dare, Szmukler, le Grange, & Dodge, 1997; Russell, Szmukler, Dare, & Eisler, 1987). In one of these trials, young patients were randomly assigned to either family therapy or "supportive" individual therapy. In another, the random assignment was to family or psychoanalytic psychotherapy. In both trials, the young people treated with family therapy had a better outcome, and this was confirmed at five-year follow-up. The same pattern of improved outcome with family therapy was not found in adult patients.

These findings have been influential (and rightly so), with the treatment of choice for young people with a short period of illness usually being family therapy. However, perhaps where these studies have been less useful is in making a rigid distinction between family and individual treatment. In ordinary child and adolescent psychotherapy services, families will always be included in the treatment of an ill child, whether or not the child is also treated individually without the family. I am not really surprised that individual psychoanalytic psychotherapy with a young person often fails if the family is not included in some way. I am sure it is the case that for these very ill young people to get well, they need the full support and cooperation of their families.

The problem with this kind of research, it seems to me, is that it is based on an idea of competition between different methods of treatment and an attempt to "prove" one kind of treatment to be superior. In fact, with most very ill young people, almost certainly a combination of approaches will be needed.

Cognitive approaches

Another approach to treatment which is often held up as an alternative to psychoanalytic psychotherapy is cognitive behaviour therapy (CBT). CBT is a short-term, structured method of tackling problems (see, for example, Beck, Rush, Shaw, & Emery, 1979) which involves patient and therapist in a collaborative attempt to identify and modify learned beliefs and patterns of behaviour. It involves a logical challenging and reality-testing of beliefs and thoughts. There are many variants of CBT, including cognitive an-alytic therapy, which integrates some aspects of a more psychody-namic approach. One can quite see why CBT or one of its variants might be thought to be appropriate in treating eating disorders where irrational, even delusional, beliefs abound. The thought that one might be able to teach an anorexic girl that the weight she has in her mind as her own ideal weight is not in fact consistent with life, or that at a BMI of 20 she would not be hugely fat, is im-mensely appealing. I have no doubt that it is useful to speak to the sane and rational part of the patient about these matters, and it is always interesting to see with each individual patient how much she is able to follow this sort of thinking. However, it seems to me important at the same time to remember that there is another, more psychotic part of the patient that is linked with deadliness and will simply not allow her to carry out these simple changes in thinking. I do think there is a place for CBT. I quite often refer patients to CBT practitioners or request referrals from the GP. But this would normally be when both I and the patient feel that suffi-cient work has been done on the underlying situation that she will be able to use it. I do think patients get into bad habits of thinking about food, and, when their state of mind is sufficiently improved, some patients find it very helpful to work on these.

A major difference between CBT and a psychoanalytic ap-proach is that in psychoanalysis we assume that a transference relationship will develop and that at some point we will encounter what we describe as a negative transference. The therapist will become to the patient a figure comprising certain key elements of the powerful, frightening, and cruel figures that the patient has somewhere in her mind and that keep her in their grip. (A good example of this is Ms C in chapter 4.) In a psychoanalytic approach we do not try to avoid this or minimize it. Most importantly, we do not take it personally, as though it were directed at us as real, ordinary people. We do not expect the patients to be friendly to-wards us much of the time, and there is no pressure on them to be so. There is also no pressure on the patients to be positive, to want to get better, or even to want to live. Our hope is that by allowing the very bad psychic situation that so torments the patient to emerge in the transference, it can gradually, over time, be modified and something more helpful can be internalized. Ms K, mentioned in chapter 8, is a good example of a patient who seemed coopera-tive and insightful but continued on her downward path until we managed to engage with a hostile and much more primitive situ-ation in her mind, initially enacted with the staff.

Some patients (and some therapists) say that they find the lack of structure of an analytic session difficult to bear. With CBT they feel the therapy to be more task-oriented, with stated goals and homework to do between sessions. For me, it is the very fact that we don't tell the patients what to do that makes analytic work so special. If we are trying to allow unconscious as well as conscious thoughts and processes to develop, we have to allow a space where anything is allowed to happen. It is not the case, in fact, that psychoanalytic work is unstructured. There are clear and firm time boundaries, and the patients are given the task of telling us what comes into their minds. I think one of the problems of working in this way is that, with anorexic patients in particular, one is often met with an overwhelming sense of emptiness and despair. This is an experience that both patient and therapist may prefer to avoid.

My suspicion about CBT is that it may seek to make an alliance with the part of the patient that is well while failing to make con-tact with the more disturbed part. In patients who are less severely disturbed, this may be effective. It may strengthen the well part of the patient and enable her to battle alone against her disturbance. However, I cannot avoid the thought that this must leave the patient feeling lonely and not understood and potentially at risk again from the more destructive parts of herself.

I am sure that CBT is a very helpful approach for people who have got into a muddle with their eating, perhaps dieting too rap-idly and losing a sense of perspective. A cognitive approach could help them quite quickly to regain a sense of balance and may pre-vent them from developing a more serious problem. This assumes, however, that the patient is not suffering from some underlying personality disorder or depressive illness. In these cases, it seems likely that the underlying problems need to be understood before there can be an improvement in the symptoms.

Work in inpatient settings

A chapter by Jeanne Magagna in her recent book illustrates some of the dilemmas in treating a very ill patient (Magagna, 2004). The chapter describes work with a 17-year-old inpatient, suffering from what is sometimes known as pervasive refusal syndrome. This is a condition in which there is a marked degree of anorexia accompanied by a psychotic depression, a profound withdrawal of affect, and mutism. Magagna, a child psychotherapist, describes the struggle within the staff group over such a patient. After "ordinary" treatment failed, the patient was given electroconvulsive therapy, which some members of the staff group thought to be a cruel treatment. When this too failed, as a last resort the psycho-analytic child psychotherapist was permitted to try to work with the patient. Some other members of the staff group considered this to be a cruel treatment, feeling that the child was ill enough without being "subjected to" psychotherapy!

Magagna describes her attempts to talk to the patient, at first superficially, but gradually with increasing firmness and conviction. This led initially to the development of a negative transference, where the therapist became a feared and mistrusted figure, and finally to the emergence of the cruel and hostile part of the patient. Magagna comments upon how very difficult it was for all the staff to see the destructive aspects of the patient. They all tended to see her as a passive "victim" of someone or something they did not understand, as well as blaming each other for being cruel to her. This is a good example of the cruel, murderous aspects of the patient being disowned by her and projected powerfully into the staff team, which under such pressure finds it increasingly difficult to function as a team. In this instance, the child psychotherapist was able to use her analytic framework to understand what was happening and to talk to her colleagues. This is a very familiar situation, but it is not always possible for the staff involved to see so clearly what is happening and that it is really about the illness of the patient rather than deficits in the staff.

It is immensely difficult for staff to be working continually with a group of patients who insist that they do not need help and, in many instances, actively resist it. A colleague of mine who was asked to act as consultant to a staff group in an eating-disorder service told me of the following situation. Although the staff had actively sought my colleague's involvement, they seemed very reluctant to use any of the help she offered. They had their own rather entrenched views about what was going on, and going wrong, in their service. The staff had a number of very difficult patients whom they were struggling to treat on a weight-restoration programme. There was a great deal of talk in the team about the inadequacies of the kitchen staff and how uncooperative they were in producing the right sort of food in the correct size of portion. My colleague commented that it must be very difficult to keep on producing high-quality food when no one wants it. Her comment was completely ignored, and the team continued to complain about the kitchen staff. It was only when the consultant pointed out that no one seemed to want her food either that they were able to share how unwanted and unappreciated they all felt. In fact, of course, the patients are highly dependent on the staff—dependent on them for their continuing to live. It is this combination of having to tolerate the intensely disturbing projections from the patients while at the same time needing to work very hard, and to be constantly vigilant in order to keep the patients alive, that makes the work so difficult. Remember that many of these patients are detained under the Mental Health Act and are under 24-hour observation, so the patients and staff are intimately involved with each other. The staff have no space at all to distance themselves from the patients' disturbances.

Carole Bowyer (2007), writing from the perspective of the dietician in a specialist service, describes the structure of mealtimes on the unit. The staff struggle to maintain an environment that offers sufficient containment of primitive anxieties to allow the starving patients to eat. Of course, they fully understand that much of the anxiety around food stems from the fact that the patients *are* starving, even though they insist they are not. Ordinary people deprived of food over long periods of time develop a preoccupation with it and some behaviour similar to that of the anorexics, such as making each meal last a very long time or cutting the food into tiny pieces. But these patients are not "ordinary". In addition to their compromised physical state, they are caught up in a serious developmental disorder in which eating feels as if it will propel them instantly into the maelstrom of adult sexuality, with which they feel completely unable to cope.

What I have discovered in the course of my work with senior staff who work in specialist services is that they very often simply do not realize how difficult the work is. I think it is often a relief to them, when they present a harrowingly difficult clinical situation, to hear the sharp intake of breath from senior colleagues who are simply shocked at what staff are having to cope with. When we recover from our shock, we can often think quite helpfully about the patients. This is why it is so helpful to have an outside view of these clinical situations. The staff who simply have to manage the work and the patients from hour to hour lose sight of what is really being expected of them and what a near-impossible task it is in which they are engaged.

Themes in psychotherapy

While the symptoms of eating disorders are remarkably similar between one patient and another, the experience of psychoanalytic treatment is a totally unique experience with each patient. It is therefore difficult to make too many generalizations. However, I think it is worth attempting to identify and illustrate some of the themes that I have encountered.

A very familiar theme is a patient who seeks to establish—indeed, has already established in her mind—a sense of oneness with the therapist. This is the relationship that Birksted-Breen (1989) describes as gradually emerging in the transference. Sometimes, however, the same sort of wish on the part of the patient can appear in the therapy in a somewhat more dramatic way.

Patient Y began her analysis full of hopefulness and enthusiasm. She was sure that here for the first time in her life she would find the kind of relationship she had always craved. She had had several other attempts at treatment, but now she was certain she had found what she so much needed.

In the early weeks she spoke little, seeming to prefer to lie contentedly on the couch. When she spoke, it was never about herself or her life outside the consulting room. She would occasionally, in very slow and halting words, tell me something about the way she was feeling in the session—for example, warm or cold, anxious or expectant—or else she would tell me of her hopes for the analysis and how at last she felt her life could come together. She often referred to therapy as being like some magical, mystical process, or perhaps a religious experience. There was an uncomfortable eroticized feeling in the room.

Gradually she began to tell me her dreams. The first dream was of *she and I dancing together, scrutinizing and mirroring each other's every move.* She had further dreams of *people in bizarre robes, perhaps like freemasons, engaging in rituals that presumably had meaning for them but none for her.* All this time, she seemed very content in her version of analysis. I began to interpret that she had come into analysis looking for a longed-for union with me, as an ideal mother–child relationship, in which there would be no difference, no life outside the analysis, no anxiety—and actually very little meaning.

The patient gradually began to understand that she and I had a different view of analysis. She felt terribly criticized and in the wrong. However, she did not express her anger and disappointment directly to me. It was upon herself that she heaped blame for her stupidity and arrogance. Her language changed, becoming almost biblical at times in her self-denigration, and I had the first glimpse of a highly judgemental and harsh version of a superego. Needless to say, this was to become a prominent feature of the analysis.

Another theme that I have found to recur in different forms is the idea of an internal object that is narcissistic. By this I mean an object that holds out great promise and may appear to be extremely special and important, but whose aim is self-aggrandizement rather than to care for the subject. The idea is of a mother who had a baby, not because she wanted and needed a baby to love, but so that she would look like an important woman, a mother-with-a-baby, the envy of other women and rather self-sufficient, with the baby almost a designer accessory. I have found that patients who conceive of their objects in this kind of way can very easily fit psychoanalysis into their preconceptions. The analyst is seen as self-important—and, indeed, what a self-important title "psycho-analyst" is for many people. It can imply that we can understand more about people than they do about themselves (or, rather, that we think we can). I think the magical and mystical powers referred to in Patient Y's dream also refer to a highly omnipotent version of psychoanalysis in which the analyst regards him/herself as being in possession of powers or gifts that render him or her superior.

Patient BJ reacted to any interpretation as though it were an attempt on my part to prove my superiority. An interpretation that actually touched her might lead to a whole session, or even several days, of suspicious silence. BJ was a patient who found it almost impossible to make the best of herself in terms of taking care of her (undoubted good) looks. She believed that any woman who was in any way concerned about her appearance was "puffed up" and "full of herself". She, in contrast, had no interest in such things. She felt her whole life had been a series of confrontations with women like myself: puffed up, full of themselves, and wanting only to show themselves as cleverer, more special, and more beautiful than she. BJ's experience of me in the transference was an extreme version of a situation that I have encountered several times in work with eating-disorder patients.

This kind of reaction to analysis may be based on the actual experience of a very competitive mother who could not allow her daughter's youthful beauty to go unchallenged, and who did indeed care more about her own position as mother, both in her own mind and that of others, than about the child's development. On the other hand, it might be based on the experience of a little girl who could not bear to have a mother who was a grown woman and, in the father's eyes, beautiful. Might the father's admiration of the mother, especially if experienced prematurely, before a secure attachment to the mother was in place, lead to such a resentment that development is effectively blocked? In my experience, one never quite knows exactly how these problems originate, and we can never have more than working hypotheses in any individual case.

This constellation of a beautiful, unavailable mother, locked into her own concerns about herself and how she appears to others, her own superiority over others, with father on the sidelines, admiring her, is a familiar theme. It leaves the patient feeling helpless and without parents who wish to help. Her plight only intensifies the mother's superiority, and with it the father's admiration. The task of the psychotherapist in this situation is not to address the "real" situation, in terms of trying to decide what the parents and the child really think (or did think, if the patient is a mature adult). Rather, our role is to enable the patient to have a glimpse of the constellation in her mind which is impeding her development. In addition, we might be able to help the patient to take a small step back so that she can gain some perspective and perhaps begin to think about herself and her objects in a different way.

The "negative therapeutic reaction"

"Negative therapeutic reaction" is a term Freud used in the discussion of patients who seem to respond to therapeutic help by getting worse (1923b). He linked it with an unconscious sense of guilt and a need to continue to suffer. He emphasizes that this sense of guilt really is unconscious. The patient does not feel guilty: she simply feels as though she must relentlessly pursue her goals, however much she harms herself in the process. As discussed in chapter 7, Freud understands this as a situation in which the superego (or conscience) has turned the full force of its destructive attack against the ego or experiencing self. A good example of this is Ms K, described in chapter 8, who, in spite of seeming compliant and even insightful, continued to get worse. It was only when the staff succeeded in understanding her destructive impulses and, indeed, experienced the full force of her hostility that she was able to begin to make progress. It transpired that K did indeed have a great sense of guilt towards her recently deceased father, coupled with a rage against both parents for what she perceived as their inadequacies.

In psychotherapy with such patients, it seems essential that the unconscious sense of guilt becomes consciously accessible and also that some of the hostility that is turned towards the self finds expression in the transference relationship with the therapist. It is not helpful to the patient for the therapist to maintain a super-ficially good relationship with her at the cost of allowing her to express negative feelings, which are often extreme. There are a number of examples of work in the negative transference in the following chapters, and I hope these will provide some evidence for the importance of allowing the full force of the patient's nega-tivity to be expressed and experienced.

This brief sketch of the kind of work I do will, hopefully, have provided the reader with a framework for understanding the chapters that follow. These contain many clinical examples, taken from my own work and from that of colleagues and students.

CHAPTER FOUR

Eating disorders
and object relations

Psychoanalytic thinking about eating disorders took an important step forward when it began to be possible to think about symptoms as representing disturbances in relationships. This is very much in the tradition of Freud's earliest formulations concerning hysterical and obsessional neuroses where the symptoms were considered as displacements of affects or ideas onto other ideas or onto parts of the body (as in hysterical conversion).

One very common example of such a dynamic in both anorexia and bulimia is a situation in which the patient is terrified of her own greed. She may deal with this by strictly and obsessionally limiting her food intake, so as to make sure she is not guilty of greediness. Or, as in the case of bulimia, she may from time to time indulge in greedy gorging, which will be followed by self-induced vomiting in an attempt to rectify the situation. Usually we will find a similar pattern in the individual's relationships. She may be a highly dependent person by nature, but someone who at the same time is terrified of her own dependent feelings. She may equate dependency with weakness or helplessness and try her best to create a sense of her own emotional self-sufficiency, refusing all help and understanding from other people. She may, from time to time, allow herself to form highly dependant relationships, but will suddenly pull away, terrified that she will become a helpless baby if she allows herself to make emotional contact with another person. The anorexic or bulimic individual may remain consciously unaware of her relationship problems, focusing her attention instead on the way she enacts the relationship problem with her food. And, of course, being obsessed with one's own body and food intake does mean that ideas about troubling relationships do recede, further bolstering the illusion of self-sufficiency. I want now to look at one very specific aspect of the object relationships found in anorexia and bulimia and the murderous phantasies involved in the attempts by the patients to control their internal worlds. Anorexia and bulimia are both violent, sometimes murderous symptoms, directed towards the self. I believe that there is also a great deal of deadly intent towards the objects as well.

Anorexia and bulimia: the issue of control

It was Hilde Bruch who first stressed the need the anorexic has to control her body, feeling that this must be to compensate for a lack of control in her life (Bruch, 1974). However, in my view it is her mind that the anorexic is attempting to control. There are certain thoughts and ideas so repellent to her that she seeks to create a "special" state of mind in which they are simply impossible. These thoughts are connected with sexuality—the sexual self, but most importantly the sexuality of the parents. Other unthinkable thoughts include those to do with development, change, growth, and creativity.

In this chapter, I argue that for all her efforts to control her weight and food intake, it is really an internal situation, a situation in her mind, concerning herself and her family, that the anorexic is seeking to control—and by murderous means. Bulimia seems to me to represent a linked and yet distinct attempt to control the internal world.

In this chapter I present material concerning three patients: Miss A, a chronic and seriously low-weight bulimic patient; Mrs B, a chronic anorexic; and Ms C, an atypical anorexic of late onset. Miss A and Ms C were treated in analysis, whereas Mrs B was seen for an extended assessment and subsequently entered once-weekly psychotherapy. I also briefly mention material from other patients with eating disorders to provide additional evidence.

The discussion focuses on the different means that the patients employ to feel in control of their internal worlds, and their possible motives for doing so. I argue that eating disorders could be considered as mechanisms that patients use to buttress manic defences against depressive pain associated with the reality of the oedipal situation. I conclude by attempting to link the symptoms and phantasies of the three patients with the varying nature and seriousness of their psychopathology.

Whenever one meets a patient in the grip of anorexia nervosa, one knows that some kind of catastrophe has taken place. Without knowing how or why, it seems that psychically the patient has given up on the idea of relationships and, crucially, on any possibility of development. It is as though, unconsciously, some kind of decision has been made. All sense of relatedness to an object is lost. The patient can hardly speak to us, if at all. If she does, she can appear flat and superficial.

The internal state that corresponds to this outward appearance is difficult to describe.

An anorexic patient in analysis, Ms C, would talk of a "white-out"—a situation in her mind in which snow had suddenly and heavily fallen, obscuring all sense of differentiation and, at the same time, annihilating all life. She loved this state, feeling that she alone knew how to survive it. The clumsy analyst would, of course, fall down a crevasse, and there she would be, gloriously alone in her white desert. The same patient would at times tell me in a dreamy way that what she appreciated most about analysis was that the analyst had no qualities, like her idea about God. To have an analyst who was a real person, she felt, would be quite unbearable.

Another anorexic patient dreamt *that she was having intercourse with her boyfriend, when suddenly everything went white.* She

explained that she loved white and often in her dreams everything went white. Her flat was all painted white.

I think the "white-out" represents an objectless world, a state of
mind where the couple no longer exists. It is very significant that
the state is white. It is felt by the anorexic to be "pure", "clean",
and hence good. The murderous destructiveness that has been
employed in order to bring about this state of affairs is entirely
denied.

I have been trying to describe the very pervasive sense in
which the anorexic patient seems to kill off a lively part of herself,
represented by the creative couple. It is this unavailability of a
part of the patient that could use help to grow and to mature that
makes analysis so difficult. In her phantasy she has annihilated all
need and the part of herself that could need—the feeding mother
who could meet the need and the creative couple who gave life
to her. In its place she has instated a sense of oneness, subtle yet
pervasive, with a featureless object, a barren landscape, a white
room, an analyst without qualities—which she feels to be far
superior to a mother or to an analyst with a mind who might be
able to meet her need for understanding. It is a sense of being
unseparated, of being at one with—but, most of all, in control
of—an object that she herself has created and that seems to have
no human qualities.

In bulimia, the symptoms are overeating followed usually by
vomiting or sometimes taking large quantities of laxatives. Patients
describe a rising of tension in their minds, a kind of unbearable
excitement, which can only be relieved by the eating and vomiting. The patients describe a sensation of sublime contentment and
relaxation, a kind of nirvana state, which follows the end of the
whole cycle.

My patient Miss A has been bulimic for twenty years. Since
starting her analysis she has become able to read, something
she had not managed since her teens. Yet the only books that
interest her are books about serial murder.

For Miss A, and I believe for other bulimic patients, the episodes
of vomiting represent a killing of internal objects, but these are

objects that do not stay dead, as they seem to do in the case of the anorexic. Serial killing is needed.

Another patient puzzled at her own terrible guilt about each episode of vomiting. She said she felt as though she'd killed someone, and she couldn't understand why it felt like that.

Although the bulimic patient may ideally wish to control her internal objects in the way the anorexic does, her objects seem more resilient and, from time to time, she is aware of her need of them. In fact, she often feels intense need, as demonstrated by her binges. Yet almost at once, like the anorexic, she hates her own alive and dependent self and the objects on whom she could depend. The vomiting represents her hatred and repudiation of the objects that, only minutes before, she has so greedily and cruelly devoured.

As in anorexia, it is not just the objects themselves that are attacked and killed: it is objects—and specifically the parents—in relation to each other.

Miss A, when she began analysis, insisted that her parents led entirely separate lives, although they lived together. According to her, they had separate bedrooms at different ends of the house. So intensely did she hate the idea that they might have any relationship with each other that she could not bear to see couples lovingly involved with one another. She said it made her feel sick. She couldn't watch television for fear of seeing a couple, and should she accidentally catch sight of one, she would resort to uncontrollable vomiting.

Her life, up until she began her analysis in her mid-thirties, had been a constant protest against the reality of her parents' love for each other. She insisted they never were together, and even her own conception and birth had not convinced her differently.

I am suggesting that bulimia represents the serial killing of internal objects, specifically the parental couple, which keep coming back to life. Such patients often think of themselves as failed anorexics. They do not have the anorexic's iron will to resist food. In fact, I think these patients usually retain an intense interest in their objects, much as they might want to deny that this is the case. Put another way, for whatever reason they cannot kill off their love and dependence as effectively as the anorexic appears to be able to do. Rather than the "clean" white-out, there ensues a series of terrorist attacks or serial murders, often going on for many years (in the case of Miss A, for two decades).

In terms of recovery, many anorexics progress on to bulimia. They rekindle their interest in an object—or, rather, they cannot resist doing so—but such an interest is feared and hated. Nonetheless, bulimia and the state of mind that it represents is a movement towards life, in spite of the conflicts involved. In bulimia, there is at least an acknowledgement of the existence of the hated parental couple.

It seems to me that the secrecy of the vomiting symptom is highly significant. (Dana & Lawrence, 1987). Anorexia could not possibly be kept a secret: its symptoms and effects are too noticeable. In addition, I think the anorexic needs a helpless object to watch her destructiveness. By contrast, in secret vomiting, the destructiveness is hidden and denied. The patient is often able to live a creative life as long as she holds onto her secret symptom. While in anorexia the problem is lived out, in bulimia it is encapsulated. It is as though the part of the self that hates life and is opposed to all contact is encapsulated in the vomiting symptom, thus leaving other parts of the self relatively more intact.

Control in the transference and countertransference

For all the differences in the kinds of symptoms they present and in the pathology underlying the symptoms, patients with eating disorders do have in common a peculiar way of controlling the analyst and the analytic situation. In very obvious terms, they frequently create such a crisis with regard to their physical health that the analyst cannot do his or her job properly or may feel obliged to intervene in extra-analytic ways, such as speaking to physicians. But even in analyses in which the patient's weight and physical health is stable, and there seems to be at least some sort of working alliance, I still believe the pressure on the analyst to comply with a particular view of a relationship is a marked characteristic. It is normally a pressure to be entirely ineffective, either by way of being an extension of the patient herself or in some other way being rendered lifeless and helpless. Of course all patients put pressure on the analyst to become the transference object, but in these cases I think pressure is often very subtle and very powerful. A further characteristic is the anxiety the analyst feels about resisting this pressure and the often catastrophic reaction of the patient when some of this is pointed out.

I would like to continue with some clinical material relating to the assessment and beginning of treatment of Mrs B, a woman in her 30s who had been anorexic since her early teens.

In spite of her illness, she had managed to marry a man much older than herself and have a child. In the year prior to her assessment, she had been admitted to hospital with a diagnosis of "restrictive anorexia". Her reason for seeking treatment at this point was, she said, not so much for her eating disorder as for her obsessive anxieties about her son. She was seen for four assessment sessions and subsequently taken into once-weekly psychotherapy.

The assessment was dominated by the patient's need to control the process and, in particular, to feel part of a couple. Her concern from the outset seemed to be about what kind of pairing was to take place and between whom. It is significant that the assessment took place in an institutional setting, where patients often anticipate and expect a pairing between the assessor and the institution or perhaps the referring doctor. Two days before her first appointment, the patient phoned to ask if she could bring her 2-year-old child. She was encouraged to make alternative arrangements, which she did, but she arrived 30 minutes late. The assessing therapist had been left to experience the feelings of being alone, not knowing whether to expect a single patient or couple, and wondering what the others were doing during the first half of the session.

In the second assessment session, the patient tried hard to form a couple with the assessing therapist (a woman). Her attitude was confiding, with an appearance of intimacy. She said she thought she might be gay and complained at length about her unsatisfactory relationship with her husband, with whom she had had no sexual relationship since the birth of the child. She spoke in glowing terms of her close and caring relationship with her mother. When questioned about father, she replied that he was largely absent during her growing up.

It emerged that the patient's husband, who had become grossly obese since the marriage, was felt to be impotent and rather disgusting—like her father, she said—and she constantly discussed with her mother and sister whether she should leave him. This situation had been going on for years.

In the third session, Mrs B's fears of being excluded were taken up, specifically in relation to the ending of the assessment and an anticipated wait for treatment with a different therapist. The patient was able to acknowledge that feeling left out was a constant problem; she could not bear to see her husband playing with their son. Although she had previously painted a picture of a close and supportive relationship with her own mother, she now confided that she always felt that her mother preferred her brother.

In the final assessment session, the patient arrived with her 2-year old and proceeded to demonstrate to the assessor what it was like to be excluded from a mother–child couple, while she, the patient, was able to shield herself from her own feelings about the separation from the therapist at the end of the assessment.

Within weeks of starting treatment, the patient had settled into a comfortable routine of telling the therapist (a man) how hopeless the husband was and, very indulgently, how hopeless the therapist was for not telling her what to do about it. The therapist reported that he felt as though he were trapped in a loveless marriage.

Mrs B had never been able to give up her exclusive attachment to her mother. She had been unable to tolerate the shift from being the baby at the breast to being part of a family in which there are two parents, each with their relationships to their children and each other. Her mental life was organized around defending herself against the pain of the jealousy and envy this would involve. In her mind, she managed to maintain the illusion that she and her mother constituted the real and central couple, with father seen as an undesirable intruder. This, in my view, is very typical of patients who go on to develop anorexia.

Although this patient managed briefly to experience herself as part of a couple, the overwhelming impression was of her great hatred of couples, both her parents and her own married state. Mothers and children, especially daughters, seemed in her mind to be the important dyad. Her hostility towards her husband was graphically demonstrated by her constant cooking and providing fattening foods for him. In the transference, Mrs B sought to control the therapist in order to reassure herself that her internal world was, after all, under her control.

Mrs B is typical of many anorexic patients who seek therapy not in order to change and grow, but in order to re-establish control over their internal worlds. This particular patient sought help not because she wanted to change the way things were in her internal world, but because something new had started to happen with the birth of her child. She found herself facing new anxieties, which did not respond to the manic mechanisms she normally employed to control her internal objects. There were new pains, such as the pain of seeing her husband enjoying his son, and knowing they had a relationship of which she was not a part. It is interesting that the child was 2 years old when she sought help. While he was a baby, and particularly during the nursing period, he could be used to bolster her omnipotence and reinforce her illusion that mother and baby constitute the important couple. But when the baby began to show an interest in his father, this must have been a frightening challenge to her. One might almost wonder whether moves towards the depressive position in the child might not have allowed some depressive concerns to emerge in the mother.

In the course of the assessment, one could observe how she defended herself against these anxieties and the worsening of her eating disorder, necessitating a hospital admission, gives some indication of the strength of her unconscious determination to maintain control. Her relentless cooking of fattening foods for the husband in the face of all medical advice seems another worrying indicator of the underlying deadly aspect of her illness. Although the problems quickly emerge in the transference, it seems unlikely that once-weekly treatment will be sufficient to allow them really to be addressed.

Patients like Mrs B often manage to negotiate very long-term, sometimes life-long, but ineffective treatment. In this way, they use the "treatment" to enable them to maintain a sense of control of their internal worlds, of which control of the therapist or setting becomes an important element. Non-analytic settings often consciously offer "support" to such patients. Such long-term and open-ended arrangements also go some way to satisfy the massive and unconscious dependency needs of such patients, while such needs can continue to be denied.

Here is another example, this time of a patient in psychoanalysis, whose attempts to control her internal parents are vividly illustrated in the context of the analysis. I shall give more detail of this patient and her treatment, to try to convey the quality of the control of the internal objects and the analyst.

Ms C came for analysis in her late thirties. Her psychiatric diagnosis was atypical anorexia nervosa. She had been brought up by a single mother, probably quite a disturbed woman. She knew little of her father, save that he had been a prisoner of war in the hands of the Japanese. She never met him. Ms C strove ceaselessly to keep her internal parents apart but to maintain in phantasy a special relationship with each. Her relationship with her father was via her anorexia, her self-denial, her prison diet, the way she pushed her abuse of her body to its limit, identifying with the way she knew he must have suffered. Mother, on the other hand, was felt to be mad and dangerous; the only way to relate to her was to placate her and appease her and make her feel important. In the patient's mind, she was very good at doing this. She could get mother to do things without mother realizing it. Her trick was always self-abasement; mother, she felt, needed someone to look down on.

The analysis took on the appearance of a serious attempt at treatment. The patient was thoughtful and intelligent and brought many painful and poignant memories from her past, together with dreams, which we seemed to be able to work on together. However, I began gradually to notice something else. It seemed to be contained in the way the patient came into the session. She would knock on my door, but only one knock and so quietly that I was always afraid I would cough or drop a book and fail to hear her. Of course, I always had to be in my consulting room by the front door waiting for her. Had I been in another part of the house, I would certainly not have heard her. Once in the consulting room, she would stand almost to attention while I made my way to my chair; only then would she roll up her coat, pushing it almost under the couch, and, very gingerly, take up her place.

I began to realize that all this was having a rather odd effect on me. Far from the neutral and receptive frame of mind I would have preferred, I found myself feeling like a rather benign headmistress with a small girl, anxious and deferential coming to see me. I also felt as though there was an unspoken assumption that I wanted things be arranged thus between us. I also realized that in spite of seeming so undemanding and compliant herself, she was persistently controlling not only my actions but also my state of mind. When I began to comment on some of this, which I did, I thought, in a very careful and quite friendly way, my patient was shocked and horrified. How could she have been so stupid as to behave like this? In a way that gave me such offence? The last thing she ever wanted to do was to assume anything about our relationship, and now she was guilty of having done the wrong thing, although she had been trying so hard not to. My patient was actually quite mad and for several days quite unreachable. In her mind I was the mad one, insisting that she behave in exactly the right way as she came into the consulting room.

What I have been trying to show with this material is the insistent yet subtle way in which the patient maintains a particular view of her relationship with me, which I am pushed to support and confirm. She pretends deference, which I am supposed to demand. I am to be made to feel superior. In fact, of course, the patient silently feels superior, as she always did with her mother. Perhaps the most important point is that as long as she and I are held in the grip of this constellation, real analytic work is impossible. There can be no real exchange of views or honest attempts to understand things together, in spite of appearances to the contrary.

Shortly after the episode described above, the patient reported the following dream.

She was dressing her mother, getting her ready to go out. The patient's brother, B, was there. He let mother wander off. The patient got angry with him and shouted, "You must think like she thinks."

She said she thought that was what she wanted to say to me: that her mother is mad and her analyst might be mad too. She said it needn't have been a dream. It could be reality. She had always to think about how her mother thinks. That's how she could get her to do things. No one else could. Everyone admired it.

Her association to her brother in the dream was of someone who seemed to have a different kind of concern for mother, not merely wanting to control her. I interpreted that there was a part of her that didn't think I was mad, that wanted to use me and the analysis in a helpful way, rather than controlling things all the time. But another part of her was frightened and wanted to shout down her attempts to relate to me differently. What catastrophe might occur if my thoughts were allowed to wander off? This interpretation produced a more thoughtful response, but also brought more of a sense of reality to the session and a little more space for thought. The patient was able to think about her brother and wonder how he managed to have such a different view of her mother from herself. She conceded that probably I wasn't mad. Had I been, she thought, I'd have been "found out" by now, which I thought indicated a little more trust in external reality.

I would like finally to introduce a piece of material from later on in the analysis, when some progress had been made and at a time when analytic breaks were a great source of concern and difficulty for the patient. In the previous session I had given the patient the dates of the coming Christmas break. She had responded by sitting up on the couch, shocked.

She began the session telling me that the holiday dates were the same as her term dates. She said the date of our last session was the date her parents had got married—or sometime around then. She was silent. Then she said she was just playing around with dates. Adding them, subtracting them . . . numbers . . . days . . . all odd associations. She said it's a funny kind of very quick thinking. I wondered what kind of thinking it really was. She said, "Isn't it thinking? What is it then? I've always done it. I've been reading Freud—the Botanical Monograph—he does it. What's wrong with that? Wasn't he thinking?

I said I thought she was mixing up dreaming and reality in her mind, hoping that the coming break might turn out to be a dream. She said she was dreaming last night, half dreaming, half awake. The same thing was happening. She couldn't stop it. It was a sort of dream *in mother's hospital, where she worked. Symmetrical—medical and surgical. Different wards and words. All symmetrical.* Then she said she dreamt about a van. She thinks she often dreams about vans—death vans to gas the Jew; the van she went back to school in with a bucket in the back to be sick in. She said it doesn't go anywhere. This isn't thinking. But Freud does it about his dream. Why does it work with dreams?

My immediate concerns in this session were with the patient's persecutory anxieties about the coming break and with the worryingly manic tone of the material. She had often likened breaks in the analysis to the ends of holidays from boarding school and being sent away from the last session like being sent back. The death van in this context I took to be the analyst of the break, the poisonous container of the sad, sick little girl. However, I think the material is also interesting in terms of the total situation.

At first any difficulty about the coming break is denied (her term dates, not anything imposed by me). But at once she is put in touch with thoughts of her parents as a couple, perhaps as a result of my assertion of an intention to take a break away from her, perhaps feeling forced to remember that I, too, am married and spend Christmas with my family. I think at this point she feels she has lost control of me in her mind and of the internal parents. She attempts to deal with the reality of my and her parents' freedom almost by a flight of ideas. She takes the meaning out of the dates, confuses dreaming and reality, tries to assert some sort of symmetry, equality, which might help her sort things out between herself and her parents, herself and me. But finally the inescapable image of the death van appears, which I think does represent for the patient the mother containing the father's penis—an image of murder and destruction rather than creativity and life.

When, in the earlier material, I pointed out to her how she was, in the transference, controlling me and preventing me from functioning to help her, she was, I think genuinely shocked at her own destructiveness. It had been her intention to preserve our relationship by not allowing any bad feelings to develop on either part. Similarly, her insistence on an analyst without qualities was more her attempt to create an analyst whom she could love unambivalently, rather than to annihilate the human features of the analyst, although that was certainly the effect she had. This is not to say that her attempts to control the analyst did not contain hostile and aggressive elements; however, to stress only those aspects of the situation would be to render too simple a much richer and more complex motivation.

What Ms C had been told of the very unfortunate circumstances surrounding her conception and birth readily lent itself to the creation in her mind of a catastrophic intercourse, though this had become greatly elaborated by her own mind. In the patient's conscious and unconscious phantasy, the relationship of the parents represented a coming together of fearful, mad, and damaged elements. While I do not think the creation of such a situation was primarily defensive against the pain of the actual Oedipus situation, it did also function to protect the patient from feelings of jealousy and envy towards her parents. These had to be faced and worked through during the course of the analysis.

Discussion

I have suggested that the dominant aim in both anorexia and bulimia is the control of the internal parents, and particularly the parents' relations to each other. By taking strict control of what is taken in, these patients support the phantasy that they can be in control of the creation and maintenance of the internal constellation of their objects and the interrelationships of them in the mind.

The internal objects, both mother and father, are subjected to violent attacks, starved, and made to suffer until they submit—and, typically, renounce their relationship to each other. Alternatively, they can be stuffed until they are hideously huge and helpless.

In my view, eating disorders function in a very concrete way to reinforce phantasies of control of the internal world. The internal world—the inner versions of the parents which exist in the mind—are built up by what is taken in from the external world, coloured by the subject's own attitude and feelings towards it. By controlling absolutely what is taken in and, in the case of bulimia, by what happens to it subsequently, eating-disorder patients feel as though this internal world is rigidly under their control.

This line of thinking derives directly from the work of Melanie Klein (1935). She links feeding difficulties in young children with the fear of dangerous internal objects. Her thinking on the control—and often murderous control—of internal objects occurs within her work on the manic defence, of which she considered control of internalized parents to be an integral part. Anorexia and bulimia, although syndromes complicated by a focus on the body, do, I believe, serve to buttress a manic defence. In particular, this is a defence organized around a repudiation of depressive feelings and anxieties, particularly those concerned with the working-through of the Oedipus situation.

Klein interestingly points to a particular feature of the manic state which finds full expression in anorexia. She takes the hyper-activity associated with mania as evidence of the ceaseless activity of the ego to master and control all its objects. In anorexia, the life of the patient frequently seems to revolve around activity that, to the external observer, seems pointless. This often includes intense physical activity, but also the massive and unnecessary scholastic overachievement found in many young anorexics.

In bulimia, the hyperactivity is directly linked to the taking in and expelling of food, the gorging and vomiting. I think that in a very direct and concrete way, the bulimic patient feels as though she is doing all this specifically to control what she feels is going on inside her.

The wished-for internal situation seems to be similar in anorexia and bulimia.

Typically, patients seek to rid their minds of the possibility of a couple, and especially a sexual couple. Characteristically, it is this aspect of the parents and their relationship which is eradicated. At the same time, there is felt to be a merging, a fusion, with a maternal object, a version of the mother but stripped of all her qualities and individuality.

Many clinicians are familiar with the projection of this desired internal situation onto the external mother and family. Anorexic patients very often talk in an idealized way of their relationships with their mothers, implying that only mother understands them and that the relationship is close and without conflict. All too often when one meets mother, one finds someone who feels enslaved and terrified by her daughter's constant demands and threats. Often she is aware that she is neglecting her other children and her relationship with her husband, but she feels powerless to do otherwise.

In one sense, the difficulty experienced by these patients is not unusual. Indeed, as a number of contemporary writers—in particular, Britton (1989)—have pointed out, the acceptance of the parents as a sexual couple is one of the most difficult aspects of the Oedipus complex to negotiate, and failure to do so lies at the root of many forms of psychopathology.

What is very unusual about patients in whom an eating disorder becomes a part of their pattern of resistance to this reality is the relentlessness and violence with which they seek to impose their own illusions.

In a later paper Britton (1998) refers to a group of patients who spend their lives trying to protect their oedipal illusions and whose aim it is never to have to face the pain of the depressive position. All three of the patients I have described in this chapter could be said to fall within this group. In addition, all three had discovered a mechanism that seemed to them to link their internal and external worlds—absolute control of intake of food, or of introjective processes—which enabled them to believe that their internal worlds could evade reality.

What I have yet to discuss is the motives such patients may have, or why they need to control their objects to the point of endangering their own lives. One of the things that makes eating disorders such complex problems to treat is that the motives behind the symptoms are not always the same. The three patients I have referred to seem to me to have different, though related, difficulties which they are trying to solve.

Comparisons between the three patients can only be tentative; while Miss A and Ms C were both treated in long analyses, the material relating to Mrs B is taken from a four-session assessment and the early stages of once-weekly treatment. However, there are important differences between the patients, which may lead on to thoughts about which are most amenable to treatment. It is these differences that I shall now try to articulate.

Miss A would often feel that she would rather kill both her parents than allow them to be together without her. Interestingly, though, such states of mind were transient. The patient had a capacity to forgive, and hence to repair, her internal world. This, I think, is reflected in her choice of symptom, bulimia, rather than anorexia. Although she could hate her objects and her analyst with a murderous ferocity, it did not have the "white-out" quality described in relation to the other two patients. Her mood and her approach to me would fluctuate from session to session, and good work and useful interpretations would often go some way towards mitigating her fury and getting her back into a more thoughtful state of mind.

Miss A's long illness had caused a great deal of damage to her, physically. She suffered from serious osteoporosis and in her mid-thirties was told she had the bone density of an 80-year-old. Remarkably, as she began to recover, and for the first time since she was 13 became a normal weight, so her bone density improved, and it seemed that perhaps at least some of the damage was reparable. This seems to reflect her psychic situation, which in spite of her deadly intent, retains a capacity for love and reparation.

Of course, in a way Miss A knew very well that her parents had a sexual relationship that excluded her, which is why she had to eat and vomit so compulsively to try to keep them apart in her mind.

An important difference between Mrs B and Miss A is Miss A's great interest in her father. Mrs B insisted that father simply wasn't there; no one was interested in him. Miss A, on the other hand, demanded an exclusive relationship with both of them, mother and father. She was not prepared to give mother up, but she wanted what mother had as well. In the transference she was extremely rivalrous with the analyst, whom she wanted to see as the unthreatening older woman, no longer interested in a sexual life of her own but safely ensnared in her preoccupation with the analysis of the patient!

In this sense Miss A had made a little more progress in her development than Mrs B. Although she hated the reality of her situation, unlike Mrs B, she did know that it existed.

Ms C, the patient whose treatment I have described at some length, is described psychiatrically as atypical. I think she is also atypical in terms of her underlying psychopathology. Ms C unconsciously believed that the coming together of her parents in her mind would result in a catastrophe, for both of them as well as for her. She felt them to be damaged, disturbed, and on the point of madness. Only by keeping them apart could she keep them alive, and even then, both were in a state that required her constant attention. Consciously, she did believe that their coming together to create her had been a terrible, shattering disaster for them both. Ms C was actually capable of a great deal of love and concern for her parents, internal and external, and her motive in seeking to keep them apart was by no means always to keep them for herself, though, of course, this also played a part. In this sense her illness is different from that of both Miss A and Mrs B.

The patients I have described seek to control their internal objects with the use of a great deal of murderous violence. The violence of the anorexic or bulimic patient towards her own body is well known and quite evident. This, I think, is a reflection of the violence that is felt to be done to the internal parents and their relationship. Some anorexic patients more than others are prepared to starve themselves to the point of death. I think it is likely that the degree of murderousness towards the self and the body reflects the extent of the murderous intent towards the internal parents and their relationship.

All three of the patients mentioned had physical and psychological symptoms sufficiently severe to warrant psychiatric intervention. Miss A (the twenty-year bulimic) and Mrs B (the typical anorexic with the husband) had both had lengthy admissions to specialist psychiatric units, Miss A for the duration of a year just prior to starting her analysis. Ms C (the atypical anorexic patient), on the other hand, although her physical health did become seriously compromised during the course of her illness, never really seemed to me or to her psychiatrist to be at risk of death. Her internal struggle seemed more motivated to keeping her parents apart, which she believed to be an absolute necessity, than towards hurting them. In some respects, she lacked the cruelty of the two other patients.

All three patients demonstrate a need to control their objects, which has in each case a deadly aspect. While this produces problems in the treatment of all three, I would conclude that Mrs B—in some respects, a very typical patient in my experience of the anorexia nervosa group—would be the most difficult to treat.

Miss A and Ms C both have features that somewhat ameliorate the difficulties. Ms C, because her motives were not primarily envious, was able to value and struggle in her own way to protect the analysis. Miss A, although at times unleashing the full destructive power of her hatred towards the analysis, had a capacity for reparation and forgiveness which allowed the analysis to continue. Mrs B, at the time of writing, shows no such capacities, and this may well be why she has chosen the option of a less intensive treatment.

CHAPTER FIVE

The sexual and emotional development of girls

There seems little doubt that the advent of an eating disorder in an adolescent girl signals, among other things, that there is a serious complication in her sexual development. In this chapter, I begin my exploration of aspects of sexual and emotional development that seem to be specific to girls. I suggest that a developmental failure in infancy has far-reaching consequences for the whole personality, and I link this with the familiar difficulties in symbolic thinking, which I go on to describe in chapter 6.

In anorexia, there is usually a marked aversion to all things sexual, which I have described in chapter 4. As well an expression of sexual anxiety, I have linked this with an intolerance of the existence of the sexuality of the parents. In bulimia, sexuality, in line with the eating symptoms, may be more varied, with periods of sexual acting out, often including risks of pregnancy. Such occurrences are invariably followed by guilt and shame, and one feels that although there may be sexual activity, it is not at all integrated into the emotional and social life of the young woman. In fact, like food, sexuality always seems something of a torment to the bulimic patient.

In terms of what one might consider to be "normal" sexual development in girls, it seems to me that we have complex expectations. Parents, and society generally, seek to protect the "innocence" and virginity of the young girl. And yet, at a certain point, it is acknowledged that this process has to be reversed. In traditional societies, girls were and are expected to remain virgins until marriage. In modern societies, with marriage no longer the standard rite of passage for loss of virginity, who determines, and by what means, when girls should have sex? Such a situation must necessarily be laden with anxiety—and one feels that some precocious promiscuity, as well as sexual inhibition, may be driven by this. A promiscuous 12-year-old, a teenage mother, as well as a girl with an eating disorder may be responding to a terrible anxiety and insecurity about how and when to embark on a sexual life.

I suggest that there is, in fact, a certain contradiction in feminine development in so far as the girl's precious inner space has to be valued and protected, but at some point that protection has to be given up. The girl has to be penetrated and eventually use her inner space as a container. The psychological processes to support such a development must be complex indeed. A much more complex motivation is demanded of the girl than of the boy. It is a function of the nature of femininity not only to be receptive, open, available to penetration; inherent also is the capacity to *wait*. (If one thinks about the demands of pregnancy, for example, one can clearly see how vital this capacity is.) The teenage mothers are seemingly the ones who lack the capacity to wait. However, it is, of course, also important not to wait too long.

Here is a dream of a young woman at university, with what appeared to be her first episode of anorexia. She had never had a boyfriend. *She was with girls from school. They are rehearsing a show. They all get a bit bored with it and start to talk and mess around. The patient really wanted to rehearse some of the sketches. She just couldn't remember her words. But no one would rehearse with her. She got furious and shouted to them to fuck off and stormed out.*

The girls were ones with whom there had been threesomes and jealousies. But they had all surprised her by finding boyfriends in the sixth form. In reality they had had enough of rehearsing, while she felt she hadn't. This is a young woman who would never normally swear, so the reference to sexual intercourse seems important.

I would like later in this chapter to look at the nature of these "rehearsals" in female development.

Meira Likierman (1997), writing about girls who develop anorexia, hypothesizes that at a certain point in adolescent development, the girl begins to experience herself as a potential container. Her body prepares her for the role of motherhood, but, Likierman suggests, there is also a parallel mental process by which the mind of the adolescent girl expands with an ability to receive the projections of others. Likierman links this with Bion's notion of reverie. This gives the girl an increasing capacity for empathy. In the case of girls who develop anorexia, Likierman observes the girls to be "in revolt" against this aspect of their own development. She speculates that this may be due to their having had to act as containers for their mothers' projections, rather than experiencing adequate maternal containment.

I would like to try to understand in more detail what it is that goes so wrong in adolescence. To do so involves us in trying to be clearer about processes of development at earlier stages.

I want to turn to the work of Melanie Klein, who of all psychoanalysts writes with most authority about the development of the little girl. I am drawing here on her 1932 paper, "The Effects of Early Anxiety Situations on the Sexual Development of the Girl". It is a rather rambling paper, lacking the structure of her later works, but it is full of ideas, and Alix Strachey's translation is beautiful. The paper is based directly upon Klein's observations of small children in analysis. She uses the rather primitive language of infantile phantasy, which can seem odd today. However, I would ask the reader to bear with the original quotations below, which I believe convey her thoughts in a more robust and colourful way than I could do by paraphrasing or modernizing them.

Unlike Freud, Klein sees girls' development taking a specifically feminine developmental line, rather than being based on the masculine model and the wish for a penis. She writes:

> According to my assumption, what she wants is not to pos-
> sess a penis of her own as an attribute of masculinity, but to
> incorporate her father's penis as an object of oral satisfaction.
> Furthermore, I think that this desire is not an outcome of her
> castration complex, but the most fundamental expression of
> her Oedipus trends, and that consequently the female child
> is brought under the sway of her Oedipus impulses not indi-
> rectly, through her masculine tendencies and her penis envy,
> but directly, as a result of her dominant feminine instinctual
> components. [p. 196]

For Klein, introjective drives are far stronger in the girl than in the
boy. This is reinforced by the receptive nature of her inner space,
something innately known by the infant girl. Klein emphasizes
over and again the role of the father and the necessity for the little girl to establish within her mind a good penis—the powerful
protective aspects of the father, which also render her fruitful and
creative. To return to the earlier point I was making of female development seeming to contain a necessary contradiction, namely
the protection of the precious inner space from possible attack or
violation while at the same time keeping as paramount her future
as a mother: "If the small girl's hopeful feelings predominate she
will believe not only that her internalized penis is a 'good' one but
that the children inside her are helpful beings" (p. 230).

For Klein, the introjected paternal penis is the basis of the girl's
superego and provides its structure. This has profound consequences for the ego development of the girl. I shall quote at some
length:

> The characteristic thing about the development of the woman's
> ego could be formulated thus: the girl's super-ego becomes
> raised to very great heights and much magnified and her ego
> looks up to it. . . . And because her ego tries to live up to this
> exalted superego it is spurred on to all sorts of efforts which
> result in an expansion and enrichment of itself . . . in her case,
> the quality of her achievements will depend upon the quality
> of her ego, but they receive their specifically feminine character
> of intuitiveness and subjectivity from the fact that her ego is
> submitted to a loved internal spirit. They represent the birth
> of a spiritual child, conceived by its father; and this spiritual
> procreation is attributed to her super-ego. . . . It seems as if it

is the woman's dominating belief in the omnipotence of her father's incorporated penis and of the growing child inside her which renders her capable of achievements of a specifically feminine kind. [p. 236]

This sense of the goodness of the internal world is constantly threatened by the fears of retaliation by the mother for the sadistic attacks the little girl makes on her mother's insides and her babies. Klein is clear that the paternal object can only be internalized following a relatively successful early relation to the mother, and I think we would all agree with this. If all goes well, the internalized benign aspects of the father act as a protection against possible retaliative attacks from the mother, leading to a developing sense of an internal situation that is predominantly good.

Another quote from Klein:

As far as the girl's sexual development is concerned, I have already emphasised the significance of a good mother-imago for the formation of a good father-imago. If she is in a position to entrust herself to the internal guidance of the paternal super-ego which she believes in and admires, it always means that she has good mother imagos as well. For it is only when she has sufficient trust in a good internalised mother that she is able to surrender herself completely to her paternal super-ego. But in order to make a surrender of this kind she must also believe strongly enough in her possession of good things inside her body—of friendly internalised objects. Only if the child, which in her phantasy she has had or expects to have, by her father, is a good and beautiful child—only that is, if the inside of her body represents a place where harmony and beauty reign (a phantasy which is also present in the man) can she give herself without reserve, both sexually and mentally, to her paternal super-ego and to its representatives in the external world. The attainment of a state of harmony of this kind is founded on the existence of a good relationship between her ego and its identifications and between those identifications themselves, and especially of a peaceful union of her father-imago and her mother imago. [p. 237]

This, then, I think, is where the problems of anorexic girls originate: somewhere in the matrix of what should have been the more-or-less benign, internalized figures of mother and father, which both protect and celebrate her inner space. What, then, are the conditions for the achievement of such an outcome, and where in the case of the anorexics may things have gone wrong?

It seems to me that one of the important qualities of the mother in this regard must be the extent of her generosity. Not only must she establish a good relationship with her little girl, but she must then permit the father to do the same, and to do it specifically with a beautiful girl. The mother is called upon to share the father, including in phantasy his penis, with her daughter.

Klein again is interesting on generosity. She says "Enjoyment is always bound up with gratitude; if this gratitude is deeply felt it includes the wish to return goodness received and is thus the basis of generosity" (1963, p. 310).

Of course, the capacity for generosity in the mother will depend upon her own internal object relations. But the question seems to be, can the mother enjoy her daughter in such a way as to feel real gratitude for her beautiful and good baby to want to return the goodness received?

We talk a lot these days about the privations of the oedipal situation, about the destructive impact of oedipal illusions, and rightly so. But here, I think, in this early work, Klein is reminding us of the importance of celebrating small children, supporting their phantasy life, which will contribute so richly to their future development. Perhaps sometimes in the oedipal triangle the little girl does need to feel that she has won. Not that she succeeds in taking mother's place with father, or in seducing the father as an actual sexual partner; but that from time to time she is the uniquely beautiful, good daughter to both her parents, without rival, and that, in her own way, she is more beautiful than the mother (just as the princess outshines the queen in fairy tales, leading in these cases to all sorts of envious, retaliatory attacks). I think this does make particular demands on the mothers of the little girls, and these are demands that it can be difficult for mothers to meet—for the demands, I think, concern *enjoyment*. Can the mother enjoy her daughter enough for generosity to develop? Here we come again to the idea of "rehearsing" which the patient dreamt about and which she felt she had not had enough of to enable her to play the adult female role demanded of her.

Klein makes much of the play of children as expression of their phantasy lives and its importance in their development. She notes the importance of dolls for the little girl, the baby that in her mind stands for the babies to come. However, I think there is also much rehearsing that takes place with mother and is also suffused with phantasy. This may take the form of grooming, hair brushing, the wearing of beautiful clothes, a sense of mutual admiration between mother and daughter. I am thinking here of something that surpasses vanity and even narcissism and contains within it the seeds of the aesthetic sense: the recognition of beauty in the other, the reflection of beauty from the other.

The patient who had the dream about rehearsing complained that although she had a superficially friendly relationship with her mother, the mother had never talked to her about sex, didn't buy her a bra when she needed one. Whatever the truth of these specific complaints, there was a sense that some important sharing of female experience had been missed out on.

To summarize the hypothesis that I am making about the conditions necessary for sexual development in the girl to proceed:

- first and foremost, a more-or-less successful early relationship to mother, and the establishment of a dependent feeding relationship (whether involving breast or bottle);
- then, as development proceeds, the incorporation of the father as an internal figure, which is protective but also creative and procreative.

I have suggested that the latter requires a generous mother who can share her daughter with the father and, indeed, her partner with the little girl.

A question that is often raised is in relation to children who are not brought up by both parents. It may well make for a more complex situation, and one that is more demanding, when one or other parent does not live with the child. However, it is important to remember that we are thinking here about mental development, not just about child-care arrangements. All children have two parents, and to some extent it will be the parents' relations with each other that will determine the outcome. Can the mother maintain a space in her own mind for the child's father, which can then be communicated to and shared with the child? As much as anything, this may depend upon the mother's own internalized parents, based on her past and present relationships with them.

Ms T had been adopted as a baby. She was intelligent, and although superficially she appeared to thrive, she developed an eating disorder in her early teens. She managed to get through college, but did not do particularly well. She never had a boyfriend, although she did have one or two isolated sexual encounters. She did, however, have some strong and supportive relationships with female friends.

In her thirties she sought help. She had a very successful career, although she felt she had not really chosen it. (She had simply taken the first job that came along and had done very well in it.) She suffered intermittently from depression and hated the thought of spending the rest of her life alone.

Ms T's early relationship to her birth mother was disrupted completely when she was a few weeks old, and it is difficult to assess the effects of such an early loss. Her adoptive mother seems to have been a warm and kind-hearted woman and later reported to the patient her delight that her adopted baby had quickly become attached to her. Ms T initially described her relationship to her adoptive father as "non-existent". She portrayed him as a pleasant but distant figure, kindly but completely uninvolved. Gradually, in the course of the psychotherapy, a more complex picture emerged. Ms T felt that her parents were not close to each other emotionally. They shared a devout religious faith, but seemingly little else. They seemed to have decided that the care and upbringing of their little daughter was entirely the mother's affair and father was never to be involved. Ms T was able to remember times in her childhood when she had longed to talk to her father and be close to him, but she always felt that this was absolutely forbidden. Even as an adult, when she phoned her parents, if her father answered the phone he would always immediately hand her over to her mother.

During the sessions when we were discussing all this, the patient reported a dream. *She was following a path, which looked interesting and might have led through some woods. Suddenly she came across an angry policeman blocking her path. She felt terribly embarrassed and ashamed.* I asked whether perhaps the angry policeman represented her father. "Oh no," she replied, almost laughing at the thought. "That was my mum!"

The dream is interesting, especially the sense of shame and embarrassment, which was associated with trying to follow an interesting path to feminine sexual development. It seems that Ms T's mother did often warn her about the dangers inherent in growing up, and Ms T was quite clear that it was mother who blocked her path. She never felt free to become really involved with the father in the way in which Klein so vividly describes, as if father, too, represented something dangerous.

This is an interesting example of a child brought up by both parents, but where the father seems to have been rather absent in the mind of the mother and where neither father nor daughter felt able to assert their right to a relationship with each other.

As I shall attempt to show in the next chapter, the failure to internalize the father and the penis-as-link leads to the failure in symbol formation with which we are so familiar in treating eating disorders.

Internal factors—factors internal to the child—can also disrupt and impede development. A child with an excessive quantity of envy, for example, will find it hard to form the sort of dependent relationship with parents that leads to the helpful internalization that Klein describes. I write more about the dynamics of envy and the defences against it in chapter 7. Here I am using an example of how excessive envy can contribute to difficulties in internalizing the parents which we so commonly find in anorexia and bulimia:

Patient Z, a married woman in her early thirties, had an eating disorder of long standing. She had managed to achieve a high enough weight at one point in her adult life to have a child, although so child-like was she that I often found it difficult to remember this about her. She controlled her weight in a very precise way, and although she constantly restricted her eating and used laxatives, she was careful not to lose too much. She had also had a period of quite serious and regular drug use, though this ceased when she married. She had done well at school and gone to university, but she never managed to have the kind of glittering career of which she thought herself capable. Like so many of the patients I have been discussing, Z lacked any sense of herself as someone who might need to develop her capacities. The idea that she lacked anything in the way of knowledge or understanding was anathema to her. The notion that she might need my help in order to achieve her un-doubted potential often enraged her, although in a part of her mind she did know she needed help and that this was partly what had brought her to psychoanalysis. Z occupied herself with a series of "enthusiasms", each new pursuit seeming to be the one that would offer her the satisfaction she craved. Using her skills in projective identification, she quickly mastered new areas of interest in a superficial way and was able to make a favourable impression on her many new acquaintances Her main aim in analysis was to be the most special and original patient, whom I would be bound to admire. She would bring long and complex dreams, which she would relate in great detail, but seemed unable to make associations to the dreams and had no interest in what they might mean. She once read a published paper of mine, which she claimed to admire and which she imagined I must have written without effort.

She openly admitted that she was envious of "everyone" and that she did her best have more than others, to avoid the painful feelings of lack and to make others envious of her. She found both her mother and father frustrating and a disap-pointment in different ways. My wondering whether what she really envied was other people with more helpful parents in their minds was met with scorn. Why on earth should she care about that? As long as she could have her lavish lifestyle and admiration from her friends, what need had she of parents?

Increasingly I came to feel that Z and I didn't really speak the same language, that there were almost no shared assumptions between us about what mattered in life or what might contribute to happiness or unhappiness. Whenever I tried to put a different view to hers, she would dismiss what I said. I would often give up, whereupon she behaved as though we had discussed the matter and I had come round to her point of view. I felt in despair of making contact with her. Then one day she came to her session subdued and ashamed. She told me of a social event that had turned into a "huge disaster". The patient had misjudged or misunderstood what kind of event it was to be. She had expected an informal occasion whereas, in fact, it had been very "grand". The worst thing was that her friends had been very kind to her, realizing how awful she felt and telling her it didn't matter. Her father would have done that, she thought—pretended it didn't matter. But of course, she said, it actually wouldn't matter to him. He never realized what was important.

I said I thought that if I was kind and sympathetic to her now, it might make her feel terribly humiliated. She would then have to dismiss me, like she dismissed her father, as simply not knowing what matters. If she allowed me to be kind and comforting to her, she would feel like a child, and that was the worst thing. She agreed with feeling that it really was the worst thing. That is what she had felt last night. Like a stupid child. She was very upset, and fleetingly we were able to make better contact. I was left reflecting that for all her hatred of childhood, she really was a very child-like woman. This failure to "grow up" psychologically is another consequence of the failure to internalize the parents, in peaceful union.

I am thinking back to Klein's contention that a failure to internalize a containing mother will impede the internalization of the father and, with that, her trust in a superego that supports her creativity. This seems to me to be the source of the huge deficiency that we can see in Z, which made her continually unhappy.

In this chapter I have focused on the particular importance to the girl of the internalization of her father. Following Klein, I suggest that this process is dependent on the successful outcome of a containing relationship with the mother. The successful internalization of the father appears crucial for the development of the girl's specifically feminine character.

Eating disorders in boys and men

While the vast majority of patients with eating disorders are women, about one in ten patients are young men. Although the majority of my patients have been girls or women, over the years I have inevitably treated some boys and young men. As long ago as 1984, I made the observation that the manifestations of eating disorders in young men seemed pretty much identical to the way symptoms appear in young women (Lawrence, 1984). My view of this has not changed, although today I think perhaps I find that fact even more surprising than I did then. One would normally imagine that adolescent boys and girls face rather different challenges, and yet the anorexic boys voice very similar bodily fears and fantasies to those of the girls.

It does seem to me likely that some at least of the relatively few male anorexics we see actually have a gender identity disorder and that their primary identification remains with the mother in a very concrete way. They are therefore responding to the challenges of development *as though they were female rather than male.* This accounts for the striking similarity to the girls in the way many of them present. A careful study of the experience of anorexic and bulimic young men is long overdue. My limited clinical knowledge suggests that these young men, unconsciously locked in a regressive identification with the mother, cannot comprehend their own experience. I am put in mind of the phenomenon of male "cross-dressers", or transvestites as they were formally called. These seem to be men who feel identified with a rather normal-seeming version of femininity, which they cannot think about. Indeed, the dressing up as a woman seems to provide an arena, a psychic retreat (Steiner, 1993), in which a particular and, I think, denigrated and ridiculed stereotype of femaleness can be enacted. The male anorexic, on the other hand, seems to be caught in a projective identification with what he perceives as a pathological sense of femaleness; this is associated with the woman suffering because she is imperfect and struggling against her own nature to become ideal. Her imperfections, in his mind, lie in her very femaleness: her vulnerability and her penetrability. In both the male anorexics and the cross-dressers we find the same familiar failure in symbolization—an almost complete inability to think about the meaning of what they are doing—as we find in the female anorexics.

Another very interesting group of young men, which perhaps runs parallel to the anorexic girls, are the male "body-builders". These are young men with a marked preoccupation with their bodies, often consuming vast amounts of food and intent on transforming themselves into shapes that seem improbable and certainly "super" human. Although this seems bizarre and certainly a developmental aberration, it does not usually carry with it the deadly quality that seems to be at the heart of the anorexic/bulimic constellation. Having said that, we need to bear in mind that body-building is linked with a very prevalent culture of drug abuse, centred on steroids, which are highly toxic and dangerous. But speculation on the links with anorexia and bulimia are outside the scope of this work.

CHAPTER SIX

Anorexia and femininity

I am returning again to one of the central enigmas of eating disorders, the preponderance of female over male sufferers. I shall be picking up some of the issues and areas raised but not elaborated in previous chapters. In the first part of the chapter I shall consider two contemporary accounts that locate the origins of anorexia in intrusion or impingement of one sort or other. I suggest that what is actually being observed and described is an internal situation, an intrusive object, instated in the mind of the patient, which may or may not have antecedents in actual external experiences of intrusion.

In the second part of the chapter, I look at ways in which the very nature of femininity—the biological and psychological given of femaleness—might lend itself to fears and phantasies of intrusion. Finally, I shall propose that the intrusive internal object so prevalent in anorexia is often linked to intrusive aspects of the patient's psychopathology and, in particular, her intrusiveness towards her parents and their relationship. I further suggest that a failure to internalize the two parents and the link between them leads to a concreteness in thinking, a difficulty in symbolization, in which aspects of the maternal function are equated with food and are renounced. Anorexia is understood as a disorder in which a failure to differentiate adequately from the mother leads to difficulties in mastering sexual anxieties of intrusion, which become concretely enacted in the refusal of food.

Contemporary views of anorexia

In considering possible causes for anorexia, the onset of which often seems sudden and difficult to account for, researchers have raised the question of hidden trauma. Over the past twenty years or so, there have been a number of reports linking eating disorders with childhood sexual abuse. In a seminal paper of 1985, Oppenheimer, Howells, Palmer, and Chaloner drew attention to characteristics shared by patients with eating disorders and those who had been sexually abused. The same team of researchers went on to describe a series of 158 patients seen in an eating-disorder service, one-third of whom had had adverse sexual experiences before the age of 16 (Palmer, Oppenheimer, Dignon, Chaloner, & Howells, 1990). This work aroused a good deal of interest, and some clinicians at that time wondered if sexual abuse in childhood was the "missing link" in the aetiology of eating disorders.

It is now widely recognized that sexual abuse in childhood is relatively common and is linked with many forms of mental illness and psychological ill health later in life. It does not seem to be the case that it predisposes towards eating disorders in particular. Lask and Bryant-Waugh (2000) have reviewed the question and have concluded that, while experience of sexual abuse is a contributory factor in the aetiology of eating disorders, "sexual (or other forms of) trauma is neither necessary nor sufficient for the development of an eating disorder. Indeed it is likely that the majority of young people with eating disorders have not been sexually traumatised" (p. 70).

While researchers continue to think about the precise nature of the link between sexual abuse and anorexia, it is likely that Oppenheimer correctly recognized similarities in the presentation of children who had been sexually abused on the one hand, and the anorexic youngsters on the other. Frequently, children with anorexia resemble those who have been sexually abused in having a terror of intrusion and in conveying the experience of having been subject to intrusion of some sort.

A quite different approach to anorexia, but one that in some ways mirrors Oppenheimer's observations, is the line followed by some child and adolescent psychotherapists who work with anorexic young people. To summarize very briefly and rather crudely, the idea is that, as infants, the young people who develop an eating disorder have been the recipients of the projections of their parents, particularly their mothers (Williams, 1997a). This line of thinking derives from Bion's (1962) notion of containment, according to which one of the functions of the mother is to receive and modify the projections of the infant. Under certain circumstances, such maternal containment fails. The child is then left to reintroject its own anxieties, unmodified and not understood. Even worse, the mother may project her own disturbed feelings into the child. The refusal to take in food is viewed as a misguided defence against taking in the unbearable feelings projected by the parent. This approach to eating disorders resonates with Bion's own work, which itself suggests an analogy between psychic processes and alimentary ones. This latter interesting and potentially fruitful approach is unlike the sexual-abuse hypothesis, being couched in psychological terms. Of course, as MacCarthy (1988) points out, incest also involves the traumatic projection of feelings into the child, and it is impossible to separate out the physical and mental aspects, or to know which is the more damaging. My purpose in putting these two contemporary perspectives together is to emphasize that both involve the idea that anorexic patients have been subject to intrusive and impinging interventions, physically, psychically, or both.

Therefore, clinicians from very different psychiatric and psychotherapeutic backgrounds are viewing anorexic patients in rather parallel ways. I think it is likely that they are responding to similar transference phenomena. In considering this claim, it may be appropriate to try to understand the position from the patient's point of view. I would suggest that in the mind of the patient there exists an intrusive object, or an object with intrusive intentions—indeed, that the mind of the patient is dominated by such an object. It is important to register this as a possibility before going on to offer explanatory hypotheses—for example, in terms of physical or emotional abuse. What the clinician (psychiatrist, psychoanalyst, or psychotherapist) encounters is the internal situation made external, as it is projected with great force into the relationship between therapist and patient. The clinician is taken to represent the internal object and, as such, is felt to have intrusive intentions. In my view, this intrusive internal object and its immediate and forceful realization in the transference is an integral aspect of typical anorexia nervosa. The following clinical example illustrates this point:

Patient F came for a consultation following referral by a worried GP. She was shrouded in thick bulky garments. It was springtime and chilly, but not cold. Beneath the huge sleeves of her cardigan, her hands protruded, strangely large and very red. I found myself feeling relieved that they were not blue. The patient sat down and tried to smile, but, as she did so, the skin stretched across her face, almost transparent. She looked like a dying child. On being asked about herself and what had brought her to the consultation, she replied that she had "been a bit silly". She explained that she has a tendency to obesity and, in trying to keep her weight under control, had inadvertently lost too much weight. Of course, school and her parents became very concerned about it all, but she explained that she had seen her GP and was eating normally again and everyone felt quite happy now. Miss F's voice was little more than a high-pitched moan. She barely opened her mouth, and I found myself talking in a low voice, almost a whisper, in reply. My enquiries went nowhere in terms of helping us to understand more fully what had happened. She was perfectly content; life was as it should be; her family were very supportive; and there was no cause of her present difficulties, other than her own bad judgement, now corrected. As our interview progressed, I became more insistent and suggested that Miss F would like it all to be so simple. She relented condescendingly, but, of course, she realized she would need further help, from her doctor and her family. Of course she realized what hard work it would be to regain those lost pounds, but at least now she had understood what had happened, and she was very determined to put things right.

I found myself sighing inwardly, fearing this would be a long illness.

Here is a patient who tells me that I cannot come in, cannot be allowed to see or understand her, while at the same time forcing me to see something terrible. She tells me that there is simply nothing to see. There is nothing in her story or in her mind of any note or interest. And yet her body, which I cannot but see, tells me she is mortally ill. If I had persisted in attempting to elicit an acknowledgement of this, the result would have been a fruitless cat-and-mouse interaction. My attempts to describe the problem and articulate the fears were felt to be intrusive, as if the very fact of having the difficulty described produced an unwelcome invasion.

The clinical presentation of this patient is not universal, of course. Some anorexic patients may present in a more openly hostile and negative way, stating clearly that they wish to have their defences left intact. Others simply refuse to talk. But the message is always the same. The patient does not want what we call "help" and she calls "intrusion". This is almost one of the pathognomonic features of anorexia nervosa. If a patient seemed genuinely to want to engage us in helping her, we would be inclined to doubt the diagnosis.

It was Gianna Williams (1997b) who first used that most apt phrase "no-entry children" to describe the feelings evoked in the therapist, or would-be therapist, by such patients. The phrase captures the sense of an object that wishes to enter, as well as the patient's defensive response. This, I think, reflects the internal situation. The analyst is immediately invited into an enactment of a situation that already exists in the patient's mind.

While this fear of intrusion is usually the first aspect of anorexia we encounter, it is also one of the most enduring and most resistant to analysis. Although it is, of course, a central feature of the analysis, it is also the central impediment to making contact with the patient.

The following dream is from a 40-year-old patient, Mrs L, five years into a difficult analysis. Having been anorexic as a teenager, she had a lifetime pattern of disordered eating and relationships, characterized by a tendency to withdraw from any kind of closeness or intimacy. At the time of the dream she had made considerable progress in her marriage and her work. Her capacity to think was beginning to improve, and she was, in certain respects, able to use her analysis. However, much as she longed to be understood by me, she still persistently responded to any understanding on my part by immediate withdrawal, usually passing the remainder of the session in silence. She dreamed that *she was in her own house, coming down the stairs. She could hear the washing machine, and there was a pleasant smell of toast. Suddenly she realized they had intruders and someone was stabbing her from behind. She screamed and woke up.*

In her associations, Mrs L linked the domestic signs and smells with her impression of coming into my house for her 9 a.m. session. She said the domesticity often makes her feel content. She finds it reassuring. (This was said with some difficulty, as though it were an admission.) What the dream seems to show is that, although the patient is feeling at home with me and more comfortable with her own life, such thoughts and feelings are felt as an intrusion. In the case of this patient, the intrusion is one that penetrates into her cut-off, narcissistic world, where she imagines she has no need of food or ordinary care. In providing this ordinary care for her, I become the violent and murderous intruder. At the same time, implicit in the dream and the associations is some suggestion of the patient intruding into my domestic, family situation. As the analysis progressed, it became clear that Mrs L believed her need for help to be an intrusion into my mind. Much as she hated this feeling in herself, she wasn't able to resist guiltily trying to find out whatever she could about my life outside the analysis.

The two hypotheses outlined earlier each proposed that women who go on to develop anorexia have been, as children, the recipients of intrusive and impinging physical or psychic interventions. I do not think it can be assumed by the existence in the mind of an intrusive object that such intrusion has necessarily taken place in the ways suggested. While it is possible that girls and women who go on to develop anorexia may have been sexually abused and/or projected into by their parents, and some of them certainly seem to have been, this cannot be deduced simply from the existence in the patient's mind of an intrusive object. Internal objects are always coloured by the projections of the subject. As Freud (1909) was the first to point out, these sometimes include malignant distortions of the external parents.

Bion (1962), in his work on what he calls the –K link, writes of the instatement of an internal object that wilfully misunderstands and strips away meaning in a malignant way. (This idea is discussed in relation to eating disorders in chapter 7.) What I think one finds in the case of anorexics is a parallel construction, the instatement of an object whose aim is to intrude, to get inside, and to hurt.

I should now like to consider some aspects of the development of female sexual identity which I think may be linked with anxieties of intrusion. I have tried to differentiate the internal from the external situation and thus open up the possibility that anorexic patients may not always be reacting to the projections of their mothers. However, I shall go on to suggest that the function of the mother in the containment and amelioration of female sexual anxieties may be paramount.

I would now like to outline some aspects of femininity that could be seen to predispose or contribute to anxieties about intrusion and may, under certain conditions, lend themselves to the instatement of an intrusive internal object of the sort I have described.

Melanie Klein, writing in 1928 on the Oedipus complex, and again in 1932 on the sexual development of the girl, emphasizes the stronger introjective drives in the girl, the strength of the oral impulses, and the orientation towards taking in. As described in the previous chapter, Klein understands the girl as having an urge to fill her inner world with good objects. This urge contributes to the intensity of the introjective processes, which are reinforced by the receptive nature of her genital, which, unconsciously, the little girl innately recognizes.

These specific dominant trends are associated with equally specific anxieties. While the boy fears the loss of his precious, life-promoting genital, the anxiety of the girl is that something will get inside and damage hers. This is the core feminine anxiety: the anxiety of invasion, of intrusion, of damage to the inside, which occurs because something dangerous has got in. This is not to say that women cannot often be anxious about loss of power and that men may not fear intrusion and internal damage. Indeed, we frequently encounter these fears. It is simply to say that the dominant anxieties resonate with the reality of sexual difference.

According to Klein, the intensity of the girl's anxieties about the inside of her body correspond with her own phantasied attacks on the inside of the mother's body. These attacks are harder for the girl to bear, as the boy has his penis on which to project his sadism, and which also confirms his potency. Excessive envy in the girl of the primitive maternal object may precipitate excessive anxiety that the damaged maternal object will retaliate and hurt her insides in return.

Bernstein (1990), in an important paper on female genital anxiety, points to the significance of the unseen, difficult-to-locate, and uncontrollable nature of the female genital. With the use of convincing clinical material, she hypothesizes that the young girl-child needs her mother's help to master her anxieties about an opening into her precious internal space which she cannot see nor readily feel.

Following Klein, we can understand the girl's orientation, not simply genitally, but in terms of the orientation of her character, as being both open and prone to introjection, but also as closed and as terrified of being projected into. Crucial, according to Bernstein, is the unintrusive but active support of the mother in the process of the female infant's need to master anxieties connected with the body and genitalia. At issue here is the capacity of the mother to act as container for these anxieties. In the case of patients who develop anorexia, it might be that the anxieties were either particularly strong or else not sufficiently ameliorated or contained by parental support. The following dream of a 13-year-old anorexic patient seems to illustrate the nature and extent of these anxieties.

She was standing by a waterfall with her four friends. They had to jump over a deep chasm. It wasn't really a long jump, and there was a rope hanging there to help them. The other four made it across easily.

But the patient didn't even pick up the rope. She didn't try to jump. She just went down.

The patient's associations to the dream were that these were the four friends with whom she made the transition from primary to secondary school. They had spent a lot of time together during the first year. After the first summer holiday, they came back with stories to tell of discos attended, prospective boyfriends identified, as well as continuing worries about the first period or lack of it. The patient, on the other hand, came back having lost more than a stone in weight. She saw her friends in the dream as girls who had managed to negotiate something potentially dangerous but manageable, while for her, femininity seemed to be represented by a terrifying chasm. It is interesting to note that help was available to all the girls (the rope-mother), but this patient was unlike the others in being unable to use it.

This was a young girl who seemed to have been unable to take the first steps, or, as she saw it, a dangerous leap, towards feminine maturity and adulthood. She just went down. Consciously, she felt a great sense of relief that her weight loss had returned her body to that of a latency child. She no longer felt in a state of conflict and anxiety. She felt strong and resolved.

For many anorexic women such as the patient mentioned above, the loss of menstruation and the curved, feminine body seems to be a source of strength and reassurance. Micata Squitieri (1999) suggests that such feelings are not limited to anorexic patients. She describes anxieties of intrusion into the body and some representations of the female body as being intrinsically fragile and vulnerable. She links these anxieties to the phantasy of being secretly male, or of possessing the qualities of the man as well as the woman, which she understands as defensive against such anxieties.

While anorexia represents a regressive wish to retain not only the body but also the life of the charmed child, overeating can sometimes express a wish to be an adult, a big, strong adult, rather than a child perceived as vulnerable and weak. It strikes me as very interesting that people who make themselves underweight and people who overeat are both trying to be strong, as they see it. The fat person literally makes herself big and strong in a corporeal way. The anorexic, on the other hand, splits mind and body so dramatically that, for her, her emaciated body is a sign of her mental strength. I think it is also true to say that the overweight woman is identifying with the loved and hated mother of infancy (who must seem absolutely huge to the baby), whereas the anorexic is struggling to avoid such an identification.

> Patient O had struggled all her life against being overweight, as had her mother, without much success. Now in analysis, she tried again and to her considerable surprise found that she could limit her calorific intake without too much difficulty and lose weight. Although in some ways she was delighted with her new slimmer body and the admiration and attention she received, she also found herself feeling increasingly anxious. Men looked at her in a different way, and it frightened her. She was horrified when a builder whistled at her and people turned round to stare. She also developed a fear of being attack and robbed when out alone; she was, in fact, a very tall woman and still not slight, but she perceived herself as very vulnerable.

Crucial here is Birksted-Breen's (1996) distinction between the phallus and the penis-as-link. The penis-as-link represents the relationship between the parents, creating the space for thought not available to the fused mother–infant couple. The phallus, on the other hand, is a kind of manic parody of the penis, through which thought is replaced by omnipotence and structure by power. It is to the phallus that these patients turn to defend against their feminine anxieties. The phantasy of possessing a male body, straight and lean, without obvious openings, is often found as an aspect of the phantasy of anorexic patients. For them, the thin, straight, rigid body they impose on their frightening feminine curves represents the erect phallus, with all its potency and force, not to say potential cruelty. For the overweight patient, it is often her sheer size and bulk that provides a link with phallic masculinity. In both cases I agree with Micata Squitieri that this phallic identification is primarily defensive against the anxieties inherent in femaleness.

Another patient, Miss D, seems to exemplify the defensive use of a phallic identification to protect herself against anxieties about her feminine vulnerability. This patient, a low-weight anorexic woman who had been addicted to vomiting for decades, was, in her own phantasy, the constantly ejaculating phallus, compulsively ridding herself of anything that had got inside her, while at the same time denying her anxieties about being invaded. (Birksted-Breen, 1996, mentions a similar phantasy in a bulimic patient.) Miss D, at the height of her illness, was terrified to wear a skirt because it seemed to her to display to the world her state of intense vulnerability.

The identification with the phallus, while primarily defensive, also functions as a desperate way out of the developmental impasse in which these patients find themselves. Identification with a threatening, invasive, and damaging phallus may seem as though it will save them from simply walking over the edge and falling unaided into the terrifying chasm of womanhood which the young patient's dream seems to picture. I also believe that the identification with the phallus may unconsciously be felt as a triumph over and punishment towards the hated penis-as-link, which comes between the girl and her mother. I shall return to a discussion of this crucial distinction between phallus and penis-as-link in the final part of the chapter, when I consider the impact of the mother–daughter relationship in anorexia.

It has been suggested by past writers that anorexia is the result of misplaced sexual anxiety. Waller, Kaufman, and Deutsch (1940), for example, describe it in terms of fear of oral impregnation. From what I have said so far, it may seem that I am following the same line of argument, with a more contemporary British emphasis. In fact, I do believe that the feminine anxieties of intrusion and internal damage are particularly strong in the minds of girls who go on to become anorexic, and that they have difficulty in using their mothers to help them overcome this. However, I believe that the problem has another dimension, which I shall now explore. I shall be suggesting that the patients themselves are often inclined to be extremely intrusive in the transference and that this has its origins in their wish to intrude between the parents.

Intrusiveness in anorexia

Anorexic patients put up their "no-entry" signs and communicate in every possible way that our interest is unwelcome, but at the same time they themselves are very intrusive. While denying us contact with their minds, they project themselves with great force into ours. I can vividly remember anorexic patients seen many years ago who have made a lasting, perhaps permanent, impression on me. On them I seemingly had no impact, or so I am to believe. I have written elsewhere (Lawrence, 2001) of the importance to such patients of controlling the object in the transference. The issue of control is discussed more fully in chapter 4. Intrusiveness is an aspect of that need to control. The patients intrude, in this instance by projection, in order to control the object from the inside. As well as this kind of intrusive projection, some anorexic patients also feel the need to intrude into the analyst's external life. Although they may feel guilty about such wishes, and may try to ignore or conceal them, intrusiveness always seems to be an issue.

> Miss D, the chronic anorexic patient mentioned earlier, who began her analysis in her mid-thirties, seemed to know from the start that, as well as my private practice, I had a job in the NHS. I do not know how she knew this. Although, of course, this kind of knowledge is in the public domain, it comes up relatively rarely with most patients. My NHS job happened to be in a part of the city quite near to where she lived. She became outraged about this, accusing me of invading her space, shopping at "her" shops, and so on. She began to "track" my journey back from "her" part of the city to my home, where her analysis took place. I would get off the underground at my local station, only to find her waiting for me, furious at what she took to be my intrusion into her life outside the analysis. On one occasion I remember feeling responsible for "forcing" my presence on her outside the consulting room, even wondering whether I could come home via a different station.
>
> At one point she "let slip" in the analysis that she had been having a sexual relationship with a man from my neighbour-

hood, whom she assumed I knew. I found myself fantasizing that it was my next-door neighbour . . . In this instance there seemed to be a real sense of confusion in the mind of the patient, and sometimes in the mind of myself as analyst, about which of us was trespassing on the territory of the other.

Closely linked to this need to intrusively control the object is the patient's feeling of being "special". Miss D had seen a number of different therapists before arriving for analysis, and she had many tales of how special a patient she had been. For her, being "special" seemed to mean that the relationship in one way or another transgressed the usual professional boundaries. With one psychotherapist she claimed to have had a sexual relationship. Another practised as an astrologer as well as a psychotherapist and had, on occasion, given the patient astrological consultations. This patient also felt herself to have been very special to the NHS eating-disorders unit where she was an inpatient for a year, just before starting her analysis. She explained to me that the staff allowed her to use the ward like a kind of hostel. She wasn't really considered to be a "patient" like the others. One of the staff members at this unit, who had been instrumental in her referral to me, provided invaluable cover during early holiday breaks. According to the patient, this staff member (who seemed, in fact, highly professional, in every sense) was really more like a friend whom she could drop in and see. Miss D claimed to find her previous therapists intrusive and the unit rather incestuous, with the same patients coming in and out all the time.

Holiday breaks were a torment to Miss D because she took them as evidence that she was not special enough, nor was she in complete control of me. During an early holiday break, when both she and I were concerned about how she would manage, Miss D "solved" the problem by starting two sexual relationships simultaneously, one with a man, the other with a woman, leaving her no space at all to miss me. When we resumed the analysis, she told me she thought sexual relationships were far more real and important than these pretend relationships between patients and analysts.

This tendency to seek to create a special relationship with the analyst, involving a breaching of professional boundaries as well as a blurring of the boundaries between self and object, is a characteristic feature. At the same time, and not surprisingly, the patients who engage in such phantasies often find the relationship, which in their minds they have created, to be constricting and intrusive.

A number of writers, psychiatric as well as psychoanalytic, have noted the particular quality of the mother–daughter relationship in anorexia. Bruch (1974), writing from the perspective of learning theory, observed the over-involvement of mothers and anorexic daughters and concluded that the patients had never learned autonomy. The family therapist Minuchin devised strategies for reinvolving what he perceived as ousted fathers (Minuchin, Rosman, & Baker, 1978). Birksted-Breen (1989) has described in detail a manifestation of this particular object relationship in the transference. Its main feature is a denial of any separateness or difference between self and object. There seems to be an intense wish to merge with, get inside, and take possession of the analyst-mother. At the same time, there is a constant protest at the intrusiveness of the object, with the hateful longing for fusion being projected into the analyst. Brusset (1998) describes a way the patients have of relating to their objects as though there were no boundary at all between them. It is as though mother and daughter share the same skin. This, I think, is a very good description, as it makes clear what an unbearable situation this must actually be.

This longing for merger with the object and the simultaneous fear of annihilation is not specific to anorexia. It was discussed by Rosenfeld (1964) in relation to narcissistic and psychotic states; it has been described by Glasser (1979) as a central feature in perversion and by Rey (1994) in relation both to borderline pathology and to anorexia.

Writers who emphasize the pervasiveness of the mother–daughter relationship also note that fathers in the families of anorexic patients are somehow absent either physically or emotionally. It is not that these are typically families separated by divorce, for usually they are not. Rather, this sense of the absence of the father seems to indicate an absence of his significance, as if there is a feeling that no one, including the father himself, knows or understands what he means or represents. In the previous chapter, I attempted to account for the significance of the relationship with the father in the sexual development of girls.

Quite frequently in the course of treating an anorexic patient, it becomes clear that the patient's representation of her family, with father largely absent and without significance, is, in fact, far from the reality. For example, Miss A worked hard to convince me that her parents had no relationship whatever to each other, each of them relating intensely only to her. In her mind, it was she and her mother who were the important couple in the family, with her father always waiting to be involved with her when she fell out with her mother. I was struck by her absolute insistence on this as fact. She would frequently tell me that they had separate bedrooms, at opposite ends of the house so there was no chance they could have sexual liaisons of which she was unaware. I came to know that I had only to mention her mother and father in the same interpretation to elicit this response from her. What emerged powerfully in the transference was her terror of being the little one, left out while the parents were together.

This construction of a state of affairs in which the father has no place seems to be aimed at protecting the undifferentiated sense of oneness with the mother. This, in turn, contributes to the avoidance of the pain and loneliness, which is an inevitable accompaniment to that aspect of the Oedipus complex which entails a recognition of the parents' relationship to each other.

Yet this defensive position is, in its own way, unbearable. It is the lack of the space that would be created by the penis-as-link in the mind of the patient that pushes her still more firmly into the familiar merged, undifferentiated relationship to mother and analyst. Although defended against their feelings of loneliness and exclusion, the patients understandably feel trapped and lacking in identity. The phallus is invoked in an attempt to provide a sense of boundary and relief from the perceived maternal intrusiveness. Birksted-Breen (1996) describes the way in which, lacking the mental structure that might be provided by the penis-as-link in the mind of the patient, a phallic organization is invoked to hold the patient together. One might consider that the very force of the "no-entry" defences represents just such an attempt to avoid disintegration in the face of the lack of mental structure.

These difficulties are interlinked and seem to compound one another. The more the parental relationship is denied and rejected by the girl, ostensibly because it intrudes upon her exclusive claims to the mother, the more she feels intruded upon. The phallic organization that she has adopted does not protect her in the way it promises, but compels her to reinforce her defences ever more rigidly. As I suggested in the previous chapter, I think it is possible that one of the functions of the penis-as-link in the mind of the girl in a more benign situation is precisely to protect her from a sense of invasion or intrusion to which she might otherwise be prone. Alongside her introjective capacities, and strengthened by her knowledge of her own internal space, she needs to know that she has a capacity to discriminate about what she takes in, a capacity that the internalized father, linked to the mother, might provide.

The important area of mental functioning we know as symbol formation seems to be impaired by the limitations imposed by the phallic defensive structure. This difficulty was described by Birksted-Breen (1989) in her paper "Working with an Anorexic Patient" and has also been remarked upon by Henri Rey (1994). Birksted-Breen understands this as a consequence of what in her later (1996) paper she describes as the absence of the structuring function of the penis-as-link. Hanna Segal (1957) describes this problem as a consequence of the failure to work through the depressive position, which Britton (1998) understands as linked irrevocably with the Oedipus complex. The adhesive nature of the mother–daughter relationship fails to allow a space in which symbols can be formed. It is the role of the father, representing the other or the third position, to come between mother and infant to create the mental space necessary for symbolic functioning to develop.

This is a difficult area to conceptualize, particularly as in the clinical situation it is not always clear what is a cause and what is a consequence. The problem seems to compound itself: the very fact of having such limited capacities to master their difficulties in a symbolic way makes the situation particularly intense. The patients cannot take a step back and think about their relationships with their parents. Instead, they seem to fall back on a series of what Segal (1957), following Klein, calls symbolic equations. In this primitive form of thought, psychic introjection is felt to take place by eating. In the same way, mother is felt to equal food rather than feeding being one of her functions. Father's role seems particularly difficult to comprehend in this constricted world of concrete objects, as it is denied symbolic significance. Often, in the mind of the anorexic patient, the father seems to become equated with a catastrophic wrenching apart of the mother–daughter couple. The shared skin may be unbearable, but separateness is literally unthinkable.

Klein (1930), in her paper on symbol formation, understands the lack of symbolic functioning in a small child as a consequence of anxiety about the force of his sadistic attacks on the mother's body. It is as though the anorexic patient remains trapped in just such a primitive and regressive relationship to the internal mother. Unable to conceive of herself as maturing into an adult woman and thus coming to resemble her mother, she remains concretely caught in the infantile battleground of the female body, originally her mother's, but now also her own. The more intensely in phantasy she attacks the mother, in an effort to break free of the "shared skin", the more anxious she becomes, and this in turn increases the need to banish all thought and all connection with reality. She accomplishes this by an intense preoccupation with her own body, which she attacks, in reality, as well as phantasy, with equal if more insidious force.

Difficulties in the area of symbol formation occur in a range of serious mental illnesses. This failure in symbolic functioning is perhaps the key to understanding why certain women find anorexia a solution to their existential dilemma, the only way out of the cul de sac of their minds. Locked psychically in the phantasy of a pre-oedipal fusion with mother, with mounting and uncontained anxieties about their feminine sexuality, their minds dominated by a figure whose sole purpose is to intrude and damage, they cannot symbolize any of this, cannot think about it or use words to try to master the problem. Typically, they do not produce neurotic or somatic symptoms prior to the onset of the eating disorder. This is the situation encountered in the consulting room: a patient who cannot think or talk about what is wrong. She simply knows that the very last thing she must do is eat, although she cannot explain why.

Understood in this way, the refusal to eat makes a certain sense. It can seem a means to have an identity, separate from that of both mother and father. At the same time, the illusion at the centre of the psychopathology—the denial of the reality of mother-and-father—can be preserved.

The following example seems to convey some aspects of the complex situation I have been trying to describe:

A 17-year-old anorexic girl, Miss E, was referred, by a somewhat circuitous route, at the instigation of her mother, herself a doctor. The mother was very anxious not to intrude upon her daughter's need to choose her own form of treatment and spoke briefly on the telephone of how secretive her daughter was and how she respected her need for separateness and space, although she found it difficult and hurtful, not to say worrying, in the present situation. What she conveyed was her sense of a daughter terrified of intrusion, and her own anxiety that she was, indeed, the intrusive mother her daughter dreaded. The result seemed to have been a kind of "walking on eggshells" position, in which the mother felt frightened and inhibited to tackle the problem of her daughter's illness with the help of her husband. Both mother and daughter seemed to be stuck in this situation, which had gone on between them for some considerable time.

On meeting the patient, I was initially surprised at the girl's precarious physical condition, which had not been communicated by the mother. This was the more surprising since her medical family might have been expected to notice the signs. It could only be assumed that the mother's fears of being intrusive somehow outweighed her more ordinary concerns. As the patient proceeded to describe her situation, she did not describe her mother as intrusive. Instead, she spoke in glowing terms of their good, trusting, and open relationship, a mother with whom she could and did share everything. She hinted that mother worked very hard and was often late home, but she cheerfully tolerated a bit of neglect! Her older brother was now away from home and her father often absent on business.

In her mind it was mainly she and her mother in the house, she waiting patiently and sympathetically if mother were late, but always delighted to see her, to share her day when she did arrive—the ideal couple, in fact. As long as mother did not try to feed, or threaten future feeding, by suggesting that her daughter was ill, she could be the idealized partner. The external mother had understood this and was trying to obey the rule that she must not try to feed her starving daughter. There seemed to be no trace in the material of the intrusive object I had been expecting. What seemed to have happened was a kind of splitting off of the feeding function of mother, which was equated with the intrusive internal object.

As the story and the history of this case unfolded more fully, a rather different picture began to emerge. Mother, although a gifted professional woman, had always been able to organize her working life more or less around the needs of her family. She may occasionally have got home later than her daughter, who was after all 17, but this was not the pattern of their lives. Of course, like all children, the patient had suffered privations, but it transpired that she was a deeply jealous and possessive little girl, resenting from the very start that she couldn't have total possession of her mother.

Father, although he did sometimes travel abroad, enjoyed a warm and passionate relationship with his wife. This was hated by his daughter. The creation in the mind of the patient of an intrusively destructive object seems to have been based upon the parental couple, perceived as intrusive and damaging to the fused mother–infant couple upon which the child insisted. Throughout her development, Miss E had had to contend with her wishes to intrude between and destroy the love and intimacy between her parents; at times she may have felt herself as the phallus, set resolutely against the penis-as-link. However, she was to experience herself largely unsuccessful in this endeavour. Finally, the intrusive aspects of the patient were projected into the mother. In the mind of the patient, it is not she but her mother who insists on getting inside and taking over. She is left in her anorexic state, wanting nothing, feeling nothing, and certainly not feeling her hatred and rage against the object of her love, whom she feels has betrayed her. This sense of betrayal is not simply that mother has stayed with father, but also that she has allowed her daughter to reach a stage of development whereby separateness seems a certainty. The patient lapses into her comfortable fantasy in which all is well and father and siblings do not exist.

This projection of intrusiveness into the mother is a very familiar aspect of the presentation of anorexia. It is a mother equated with food itself, and felt to be controllable by controlling the intake of food. It was the sense of concern and helplessness, produced by such a projection into the mother described above, that was binding mother and daughter together so successfully and dangerously at the time of the referral. It was mother in her maternal function as feeder, as breast, that was here felt to be intrusive. As long as mother could be experienced as part of the patient, all was well, but should the mother assert her separate identity, perhaps in the cause of saving her daughter's life, this would have been an intolerable intrusion. The cardinal rule, which this mother had correctly understood, was that she must not on any account attempt to feed her starving daughter. The child had, in fact, made herself almost the sole object of her mother's attention and helpless concern and was, for the first time, in danger of realizing her unspoken ambition to oust her father from his place with mother.

What seems to be lacking in the minds of anorexic patients is the capacity for what Freud termed "bisexuality", which is so necessary for successful social as well as emotional and sexual functioning. Anorexic patients frequently lack any identification with the father, having instead only the hollow phallus to fall back on. This attacks both feminine and masculine creativity. The failure to internalize a father, in the sense of culture and the world outside, contributes to the difficulties these patients have in establishing a working life, despite their astonishing scholastic achievements. Miss A, in spite of some potential talents, found it quite impossible to make a life for herself in the world. In this regard it is notable that in her desperation during the long break, she turned to a concrete bisexuality—simultaneous sexual relationships with a man and a woman—as if to try to compensate for the lack of the psychic structure that the internalization of both her parents may have afforded her.

To conclude, I would like to return to the links between femininity and anorexia and, in particular, the large preponderance of female sufferers. The girl's orientation towards introjection, and its attendant anxieties, does seem to be significant in a disorder organized around a refusal to take in. However, this would appear to be only part of the story. The other facet of the problem appears to be what we might term a psychic homosexuality, in which the primitive tie to the mother remains in phantasy unbroken. Nothing is taken in in a normal way by eating or by intercourse. Instead, a kind of symbiosis is imagined, which is both ruthlessly demanded but also feared. I have suggested that this can be understood as a developmental failure in which, rather than using the mother to help her overcome anxieties, the girl uses the relationship with her mother to deny the anxieties. Mother becomes a shield rather than container. The psychic consequences of the failure to internalize the penis-as-link are profound and include the familiar "no-entry" defences as well as problems with symbolization. This latter difficulty makes it impossible for the patient to find any space at all to think about the possible meaning of her symptoms, which is a serious complicating feature in the analytic work.

I have suggested that the familiar story of environmental impingement in these patients may, in fact, conceal a more complex one. Intrusiveness always seems to be an issue, but this does not necessarily originate with mother (as the maternal-projection theorists assume) or father (as the sexual-abuse believers imply). Our starting point clinically is the presence of an intrusive internal object.

CHAPTER SEVEN

Life and death

A patient dreamt of *a scene where a condemned person, hooded, stood waiting for execution. There seemed to be a group or a society in charge of the business who kept changing their minds. At one moment the condemned person would be told they were to be freed, the next moment that the execution was to proceed. It was a cruel torture. The patient felt he was being forced by the people in charge to be the witness.*

What the patient was "witnessing", in the form of his dream, was a situation in which his "self" was held at the mercy of an organization, a society—in reality, other parts of his own mind.

In this chapter I examine the psychoanalytic idea of the death drive, with the aim of testing its applicability to clinical situations concerning patients with eating disorders. While Freud sees the death drive as an innate force, parallel with the life force or libido, others have taken the view that destructive and self-destructive impulses arise as a result of environmental influences. Sometimes these opposing views take on a philosophical tone, as though it is the attitude to life of those holding the views which is at issue. I am concerned in this chapter with finding ideas that are clinically useful and enable the clinician to think more effectively under the enormous pressure that the patient's behaviour imposes.

Bion (1956), writing about the development of schizophrenic thought, talks of a "conflict that is never decided between life and death instincts". I suggest that this conflict is also in evidence in work with anorexic and bulimic patients.

This idea of a death instinct or drive originates in Freud's *Beyond the Pleasure Principle* (1920g) He further clarified it in *Civilization and Its Discontents* (1930a). This is what he actually wrote:

> Starting from speculations on the beginning of life and from biological parallels, I drew the conclusion that, besides the instinct to preserve living substance and to join it into ever larger units, there must exist another, contrary instinct seeking to dissolve those units and to bring them back to their primeval, inorganic state. That is to say, as well as Eros there was an instinct of death. The phenomenon of life could be explained from the concurrent or mutually opposing action of these two instincts. It was not easy however to demonstrate the activities of this supposed death instinct. The manifestations of Eros were conspicuous and noisy enough. It might be assumed that the death instinct operated silently within the organism towards its dissolution, but that, of course, was no proof. A more fruitful idea was that a portion of the instinct is diverted towards the external world and comes to light as an instinct of aggressiveness and destructiveness. In this way the instinct itself could be pressed into the service of Eros, in that the organism was destroying some other thing, whether animate or inanimate, instead of destroying its own self. [1930a, pp. 118–119]

We can see that from the start this seems to have been for Freud a more complex idea than that of the life-preserving instinct. He regards it as "operating silently" in terms of destructive intentions towards the self, while taking on the same conspicuous and noisy manifestations when directed outwards towards others and the world. In fact, in the case of the very ill patients I describe later in this chapter, I think we can see that it is the conflict between the wish to live, grow, and develop and the wish to regressively drop back into something inorganic which produces the conspicuous and noisy manifestations that are so frequently found in adolescent and specialist eating-disorder units.

Segal (1997) suggests that while Freud described the death drive in biological terms, one could equally well formulate the conflict between the opposing instincts in purely psychological terms. She writes:

Birth confronts us with the experience of needs. In relation to that experience there can be two reactions, and both, I think, are invariably present in all of us, though in varying proportions. One, to seek satisfaction for the needs: that is life-promoting and leads to object seeking, love, and eventually object concern. The other is the drive to annihilate: the need to annihilate the perceiving experiencing self, as well as anything that is perceived. [p. 18]

Later, she writes:

I think that the destructiveness towards objects is not only a deflection of self-destructiveness to the outside, as described by Freud—important though that is—but that also from the very beginning the wish to annihilate is directed both at the perceiving self and the object perceived, hardly distinguishable from one another. [p. 18]

Here Segal is bringing destructiveness and self-destructiveness together. It is not so much, as Freud suggests, that the death drive is deflected outwards in the form of aggression, but that the drive itself is directed against both the perceiving self as well as what is perceived, "hardly distinguishable from one another", she says. The impulse is to annihilate both. This will become clinically relevant when we consider the question of whom or what is being attacked in the case of anorexia.

Freud writes of the fusion of the death drive with the life-preserving drive, which renders it less harmful. I think this is a potentially very helpful idea. I think what we are seeing with young people with serious eating disorders is a degree of de-fusion of the death drive from the libido. Sometimes there seems to be almost nothing in the patient which is on the side of life. I believe that the developmental demands of adolescence can in some individuals produce such an effect. But this is also a potentially hopeful idea; if drives can become de-fused, they can also become re-fused, and I believe that this is exactly what happens as the ill young patient recovers. What we find is that with help and support, she begins to try out aspects of life again and, correspondingly, the destructiveness appears to diminish. The danger with the anorexic patients is that under pressure they agree to gain weight, but the internal situation remains unchanged and they very quickly begin again their relentless attacks upon themselves. Until the death drive comes more under the sway of life and love, they really cannot do otherwise.

Feldman (2000) makes an important contribution to the debate by producing interesting evidence to suggest that in the case of many patients, the death drive does not, in fact, impel them towards their actual death or that of their objects. Instead, the unconsciously desired situation is one in which self and objects are held in a damaged and weakened state, for ever dying, as Feldman writes (2000, p. 56). This he links with Betty Joseph's paper on addiction to near-death (Joseph, 1982). This again seems highly pertinent in the case of the patients we are studying. If human beings are really intent upon killing themselves, it is nearly impossible to stop them. This is part of the horrifying reality of everyday life in mental hospitals and prisons. In the case of anorexic patients, although some do kill themselves, many more spend months and years enacting their conflicts, remaining chronically ill, though alive. We could see the inpatient units as the arenas that society provides to allow these highly disturbed youngsters to work through the conflict between the life and death drives and, hopefully, to resolve the situation and move on.

Klein understands that from the beginning of life, the infant needs to take in good experiences from the environment to combat the power of the death drive. She links it with the primal process of introjection, in which the infant takes in good experiences—first and foremost food—to counteract the effects of the destructive drives working within. For Klein it is very much a matter of the balance of forces within the personality. If development goes well, the infant will accumulate a preponderance of good experiences and feelings and ultimately will internalize aspects of the parents which support its development. In the case of young people who develop an eating disorder, it seems clear that no such supportive internal situation exists. I shall now try to understand what exists internally in its place and to discuss what can be known about how it comes to be.

In 1923, Freud wrote of a situation in which a part of the self can be opposed to the self:

> If we turn to melancholia first, we find that the excessively strong super-ego which has obtained a hold upon consciousness rages against the ego with merciless violence, as if it had taken possession of the whole of the sadism available in the person concerned. Following our view of sadism, we should say that the destructive component had entrenched itself in the super-ego and turned against the ego. What is now holding sway in the super-ego is, as it were, a pure culture of the death instinct. [Freud, 1923b, p. 53]

Freud's use of words is very interesting and highly appropriate to instances of self-starvation. One clearly feels that the anorexic patients are at the mercy of something terrifyingly powerful and malignant, which is holding sway.

In the case of the relatively healthy individual, one might envisage the superego as a more or less benign construct that could strengthen and support the efforts of the ego to comprehend reality and make judgements based upon it. However, in the version of the superego described above, it would seem that the superego is committed not to the survival and development of the self, but to its destruction. This situation is vividly enacted in cases of serious eating disorder, where patients are literally commanded by something within themselves to ignore their starvation and exhaustion, to undertake never-ending feats of exercise, ever more demanding regimes. It is as also as if they are commanded not to fraternize with the enemy—that is, those around them who seek to stand up for the self and save it from destruction.

Destructive narcissism

A line of thinking that develops from idea of a death drive is the thinking concerning narcissistic states of mind. Freud writes about this sort of narcissism in his paper on obstacles to successful analysis, "Analysis Terminable and Interminable" (1937c), but he first described narcissism many years earlier in his paper on Leonardo (Freud, 1910c). In this he describes narcissistic relationships as those in which the subject takes himself as his love object. In the case of Leonardo, he loved his young apprentices—who represent his youthful self—as he felt his mother had loved him as a child. In this way, part of the mind of Leonardo is projected into the young men, while another part of him identifies with his mother.

It was Rosenfeld (1964), who drew attention to the role of narcissism in denying the separateness between self and others. The excessive use of projective identification produces a sense of merging or fusion with the object. This has the effect of making dependence on the object impossible. This would clearly be the case for Leonardo. He could love the boys, representing his young self, but he had no need to depend upon them. He had taken upon himself all the attributes and capacities of the mother, including her capacity to feed. Rosenfeld points out that refusing to depend does away with the anxiety about loss or frustration, of not having needs met. It also entails a denial of the goodness of the object, a failure to value it. Rosenfeld suggests that this kind of omnipotent denial of need and vulnerability also defends against envy. If the subject himself has all the desirable attributes, there is nothing at all to be envious of. As we shall see, the acknowledgement of envy often plays an important part in recovery from anorexia and bulimia.

In a later paper, Rosenfeld (1971) describes the way in which destructive aspects of the personality, which prevent the needy dependent part of the patient from obtaining help, themselves become idealized. This process, the idealization of the elements that are opposed to dependence and help, is a highly destructive one. In analysis or psychotherapy, it leads to a sense of superiority, often expressed quite subtly, towards the therapist. In the example below, of a patient in hospital, it leads to a sense of triumph against the therapeutic team when destructive trends win out. At this point, the analyst or team is felt to be equated with the vulnerable and dependent part of the patient (in our sense, the more ordinary and less ill part of the patient), which is to be overruled and punished for its weakness. If the analyst or some member of the team were to be allowed to make contact with the ill patient, this would bring forth a tremendous anxiety, envy, and shame about what had been going on. These destructive elements put up powerful resistance to such a recognition and confrontation with reality.

Rosenfeld (1971) points out that the destructive elements can seem highly organized, and this organization he likens to a gang. He says:

> The destructive narcissism of these patients appears often highly organised, as if one were dealing with a powerful gang dominated by a leader, who controls all the members of the gang to see that they support one another in making the criminal destructive work more effective and powerful. . . . The main aim seems to be to prevent the weakening of the organisation and to control the members of the gang so that they will not desert the destructive organisation and join the positive parts of the self or betray the secrets of the gang to the police, the protecting superego, standing for the helpful analyst who might be able to save the patient. [p. 174]

Death constellation and trauma

Hyatt Williams (1998), working as a forensic psychiatrist as well as a psychoanalyst, describes what he calls a "death constellation", a constellation of fears, fantasies, and preoccupations with death which he first found prevalent in the minds of individuals who have committed murder. He goes on to consider that the same constellation is probably also to be found in the minds of all individuals who attack life-processes, whether in themselves or others. This, in my view, certainly includes eating-disorder patients. I have shown in chapter 4 that both anorexia and bulimia appear to have murderous phantasies—usually unconscious—underlying them and that both kinds of pathology involve attacks upon the parents in the mind of the patient. In addition, many of the patients we see have a quite conscious involvement and preoccupation with death.

Williams relates the presence of the "death constellation" to a number of factors. Many of the murderer patients he treated had suffered severe trauma at the hands of their parents or others.

Sometimes the victims of the murders resembled or in some way stood for the person responsible for the abuse. In other cases, the patients had not been the victims of actual physical abuse, but Williams felt that they had become the recipients of murderous projective identification from a parent, while the other parent was unable to contain the child's own projections. This might be imagined to leave the individual with a sense of being filled with what Bion terms "nameless dread", linked to a terror of annihilation. I shall say more about this later. He also notes that in the history of his patients there are often a number of "accidents" in which someone has died.

We find many instances of anorexia nervosa in the third generation of Jewish Holocaust survivors. In my experience of working with these young people, they often feel filled up with death, even though for their parents they consciously represent the hope of new life for the family.

One second-generation patient, a baby born in this country at the end of the war, knew that at the time of her birth, her parents were receiving almost daily telegrams from the Red Cross, informing them of yet more and more members of the family who had been murdered in concentration camps across Europe. Finally, they found they were the only survivors. One can only imagine the effects of the uncontainable grief that surrounded the coming into life of that baby. And remember: both parents had lost everyone. There was absolutely no one who could help. It would be most surprising if some at least of the grief, terror, and guilt were not projected into the infant.

Another patient, the granddaughter of Holocaust survivors, was brought up in deliberate conscious ignorance of what had happened to her family. Her parents were determined that her childhood should not be burdened with the tragedy of the past, as they felt theirs had been. She developed very serious anorexia in her early teens, which, of course, was a terrible spectacle to witness for a family that had barely survived starvation. What transpired quite quickly in her analysis was her absolute hatred for and terror of her surviving grandmother. The patient felt her to be an evil witch, damaged and crazy, but she didn't know why she felt this or how it really related to the old lady who was so passionately fond of her. During the course of her treatment, her anxiety lessened enough for her to develop some curiosity about her family history. The truth was told, and it was, I think, a healing experience for the family.

Another group who suffer more than their share of serious eating disorders are immigrants from the Indian sub-continent. It is often not remembered that many of these families came to this country as traumatized refugees, following the harrowing events surrounding the partition of India, when many people were brutally murdered, villages burned, and hundreds of thousands of families left fleeing for their lives. They brought the undigested memories of these events with them to a new country, where people neither knew nor cared what had brought them here. They did the best they could, but such families are very vulnerable to breakdown, mental illness, and probably domestic violence too. They are vulnerable, as well, to the instatement of a "death constellation" in the minds of some of the members.

The important problem that these families share is not the fact that there have been deaths; all families have deaths, and death is a vital aspect of family life. The problem is that the deaths are perceived as so unbearably traumatic, and the situation so fragile and unsafe, that mourning is not possible. It is unmetabolized death—death that is unthinkable, impossible to talk about—that seems to find its way into the minds of some young people.

Fonagy (1999) writes about a possible mechanism by which trauma may be transmitted across generations. His work is based on the psychoanalytic treatment of a third-generation Holocaust survivor (the grandchild of an actual survivor). He suggests that disorganized attachment behaviour in infancy as a consequence of a frightened or frightening caregiver may leave a child vulnerable to dissociative states. In such cases, trauma–related ideas may be taken in from the parent, but in an unintegrated way, such that they cannot be properly thought about or understood.

Having mentioned this group of patients whose difficulties seem to have their origins in external trauma of some sort or another, I now want to consider patients who may have quite fortunate external lives, but who may have a long and difficult struggle with unfortunate internal factors.

M is a 23-year-old with ten-year history of anorexia. She also vomits and cuts and has made some suicide attempts. She has had admissions to several specialist units in her part of the country. She is currently an inpatient in a very established and experienced unit, with highly qualified staff. This admission has so far lasted for twenty weeks. Her physical condition deteriorated early in the admission, with abnormal blood results showing signs of liver failure. She was placed on one-to-one observation and fed by nasogastric tube, both of which have continued. She has gained at most 2 kilos during this admission. The staff do not know exactly how she is managing to restrict or vomit, but they know that she is. They call it "using behaviours".

M has extremely poor relationships with the other patients. She is highly competitive with them and claims that being on the unit with them makes her worse. Before she was put on tube feeding, she frequently tampered with the other patients' food, putting her food onto their plates. She currently shares a bed bay with another patient who is similarly on close observation and tube feeding, about whom she complains loudly, saying that this patient is a bad influence on her.

The patient is spending her time at the moment trying to subvert her treatment. She has managed to establish that she has a BMI of 12 (not high!), but the staff are of the opinion that it is probably nearer to 10. She looks as though she is dying. At any opportunity she will try to isolate a member of staff (the dietician, for example) and try to get that person to comply with giving her less. The normal topic of discussion with her key worker nurse is a barrage of requests for more exercise, visits out, refusals to sit down during the session, demands for windows to be opened, etc. etc. Unusually for a patient who is so physically compromised, she sleeps well without medication. The staff have therefore decided to limit the night-time observations. The patient has complained about this, saying that she might well start "using behaviours" at night-time.

The patient herself seems both drawn towards death and also terrified of it. She pits herself against one of the best specialist psychiatric teams in the country, trying to kill herself, with only them to stop her. They suggest stopping the night-time observations, and I think it frightens her. I think she probably is very frightened of death, and her determination to stay close to death is actually a way of trying to control this.

Bion writes of the fear of dying as though it might be a common experience in the infant. The role of the mother is to take in and process this fear of dying, to understand it, and to give it a name. Both infant and mother are strengthened, as is the bond between them, by the understanding of this understandable fear.

If, on the other hand, this ordinary fear of dying is not understood, and if the distress is not taken in by the mother, the infant is left with a terror that it perceives as not understandable (Bion's *nameless dread*). This, I think, might come close to the situation in which the seriously ill anorexic finds herself and which she desperately needs to have understood by the staff. However, Bion (1962) goes on to describe another situation that can occur which makes such understanding impossible.

He first of all describes what he calls the K (knowledge) link. This is the relationship between mother and infant, or analyst and patient (container and contained), in which mutual growth and development of the personality is possible. He says it "provides the basis of an apparatus for learning by experience" (p. 92).

He then goes on to describe the complete and terrifying reversal of this process, which he terms –K. This –K denotes a link between mother and infant, container and contained, analyst and patient, which is experienced as a continual attack on any sense of shared meaning. Both container and contained experience the other as stripping away meaning from the encounter in a malignant way and, instead of offering back a shared sense of an emotion understood, forcing back a worthless residue of what might have been a relationship. He further states that the real terror and hatred is reserved for anything that might look like development, which might represent a new idea or a new way of looking at things.

Although Bion had in mind a situation in infancy and a situation in the consulting room, I think it must be something of this order that is taking place between the very ill patient described above and the team who are trying to look after her. She perceives herself and her intentions as *absolutely* misunderstood. She does not perceive her attempts to lose even more weight as destructive, and she does not believe that the staff genuinely do either. Rather, she feels herself surrounded by objects who are completely opposed to even trying to understand her point of view and who mistreat her in ways that threaten her very existence. Certainly, the food that they force into her does not seem like sustenance to keep her alive and enable her to grow, but simply a "worthless residue", as Bion describes.

Similarly, the staff feel that the patient wilfully and malignantly misunderstands what it is they are trying to do. They are employed by their organizations to keep the patient alive so that she might, over time, change and want to live. They may feel they owe it to our society, our common culture, to try to help these terribly troubled young people to find a life. Above all, they themselves may have a loving disposition and a wish to repair damage rather than cause it. And yet they are perceived as the problem rather than as a possible aspect of a solution to the problem and a move forward in development. What is so very striking here is the concreteness with which these psychological processes are evident within the institutional setting.

So here we have a situation in which both "sides" see themselves locked in combat with another who totally and wilfully misunderstands their behaviour and intentions. Bion himself poses the question as to what brings this terrible attack on development about. His answer is one word: envy. He is thinking here of the infant's envy of the mother, or the patient's envy of the analyst. I want to look carefully at the role of envy, although I shall return to the –K link and suggest that envy might be one of several factors involved.

Envy and defences against it

Envy can play a part in the genesis of many serious mental illnesses, including eating disorders. It may seem surprising that
I include a discussion of envy in the context of the death drive
and those parts of the personality that are opposed to growth and
creativity. But while most of us are familiar with envy, both in ourselves and in our observations of others, we may underestimate
the importance it can have in undermining crucial relationships
and in impeding the development of the individual's character. In
particular, it interferes with the capacity of the individual to form
trusting and dependent relationships, a difficulty highly characteristic of those who develop an eating disorder.

It was Melanie Klein who recognized the destructive power
of envy and who located it firmly as a manifestation of the death
drive. It is associated with the death drive because it attacks and
undermines potentially loving relationships. Envy, in effect, trans-
forms love into hate. She sees the innate conflict between the life
and death drives operating from the very beginning of life. For
her, if development is to proceed, it is necessary for the infant
to establish in its mind an image of its mother which is, on the
whole, loving and supportive. She describes the way in which this
comes about by repeated good experiences, initially in relation to
the feeding relationship and the first contact the baby has with the
mother's breast.

The inevitable frustrations that arise in all human relationships
lead the infant to experience the mother and her breast as bad
from time to time. Initially, the immature ego of the baby splits the
mother/breast into good and bad, so that the experiences of the
good mother are not damaged by the bad and frustrating experiences. However, if envy plays a part in the developing relationship, it will be the good aspects of the mother that are resented and
attacked. The mother's capacity to feed and care for the infant will
itself become a source of envy. Such infantile envy is highly pathological, and fortunately it is probably unusual. A very high degree
of envy will lead to serious difficulties in the early mother–infant
relationship and may well be a factor in situations where there
are significant feeding difficulties and a "failure to thrive". In less

serious cases, the envious infant will feed, but will devalue the experience and feel no gratitude.

In adolescence and adulthood, we can see the effects of excessive envy and, in particular, the defences employed against feeling it. While all people have envious feelings towards others whom they regard as possessing qualities that they lack, the people who go on to develop eating disorders often find their own envious feelings very difficult to tolerate. While it may be painful to be confronted by the success of another and to feel a sense of lack and inadequacy, it is part of our relation to reality to be able to acknowledge our feelings, at least to ourselves, and not be too undermined by them.

Defences against envy

Envy is a painful feeling, perhaps one of the most painful to which human beings are prone. An acknowledgement that one feels another to possess special gifts and qualities, and, further, that one hates the other for it, involves the acceptance of guilt for such a reaction. While infants and small children are not able to cope consciously with such demands, they nonetheless suffer terrible anxieties in relation to the attacks that, in their minds, they have made on the mother and her creativity.

Throughout life, there is a tendency for the ego to defend itself against the pain of envy, to keep it unconscious. One very common way of denying and not feeling envy is by the denigration of the person who would otherwise be an object of admiration and hence envy. Sometimes such denigration is not entirely obvious.

A patient repeatedly referred to her therapist as a rather saintly figure who had given up all chance of worldly success in order to pursue her chosen profession. Power and money were judged to be unimportant to her—unlike the patient, who came from a powerful and wealthy family. In fact, the therapist was a psychoanalyst of some standing within the profession, but the patient had somehow kept herself from knowing this. When she finally allowed herself to find out, both she and the therapist had to deal with the full force of her envious attacks.

Another way of denying the reality of envy is to idealize the envied person. The other is held in such unrealistically high esteem that the subject cannot even compare herself to that person. This is the way in which we manage to maintain certain celebrities or stars in such high esteem without hating them for their success. The subject never feels hateful towards the idealized person that someone so admired has qualities that she herself doesn't possess. This is the position in which patients with eating disorders sometimes attempt to hold their mothers or their therapists or their nurses, although almost inevitably this eventually breaks down.

One of the most common defences against feeling envious is to project the envy—to imagine that others are envious or to set out to make others envious. In many respects, this defence against envy is a rather obvious feature in eating disorders: needing to be the thinnest certainly suggests a child who is envious of others and who cannot tolerate that envy. Scholastic overachievement also suggests children who cannot bear others to be "better" than they. The single-mindedness with which anorexic adolescents pursue their academic goals has a different quality to it than the usual competitiveness between children—which might also be based on envy. They work and study as though on a treadmill, without obvious satisfaction and in such a way as to obliterate the knowledge of what others are doing and what is going on around them. Thus the activity is not *felt* to be driven by envy. Instead, the individual feels herself simply to be very special, with special qualities of her own, not comparable with others. It is a kind of self-idealization. Paradoxically, many children who go on to develop serious eating disorders are, originally, considered enviable by their peers. They are often highly competent intellectually, thin (of course), but in addition they often have a quality of self-containedness, seeming not to need others, not to suffer the insecurities and self-doubts normal for their age. In fact, of course, the very reverse is true. The problem is that they cannot allow themselves to use other people to obtain reassurance in an ordinary way. Instead, a kind of reassurance is gained by appearing not to need any help.

Elizabeth Spillius (1993), in her very interesting account of different kinds of envy, looks at the nature of the giving/receiving relationship. She suggests that some of the difficulties that occur in the process of receiving—whether it is food, other kinds of care, or help—may lie in the way in which it is perceived to be offered. If the recipient perceives the giver to be offering something in a generous and sympathetic frame of mind, with genuine concern for the well-being of the other, although some envy may be stimulated it is also possible that appreciative feelings will also be evoked. This may enable the envious feelings to be acknowledged and eventually worked through. A sense of gratitude may eventually develop.

If, however, the recipient perceives the giver to be acting in a reluctant, grudging, and perhaps hostile way, this may increase a sense of envy, but also of greed, as if in determination to get as much gratification as possible from this richly endowed but ungenerous object.

Another possible perception on the part of the receiver is that the giver is interested not in the receiver, but in being seen as the one who has much to give. In other words, the giving is a narcissistically motivated activity, rather than one of concern for the well-being of the other. If such a perception exists in the mind of the recipient, it may be very difficult for enjoyment and appreciation to develop. The recipient may feel that although a lot of food, or a wealth of interpretations, is being offered, in another sense nothing is being given.

Mr B saw his analyst as a clever but vain and narcissistic creature. He imagined her as having become a psychoanalyst in order to prove her superiority over others. Specifically in relation to himself, he heard interpretations as her way of showing him how insightful she could be, in order to underline to him his own inadequacy. With such a negative perception of his analyst's intentions it was difficult for Mr B to feel anything but envy, humiliation and a desire to spoil whatever was offered.

The following dream seems to indicate the position he felt himself to be in: the patient dreamt *that he was led—against his will, he thought—to a place in some woods where a large banquet was laid out. It consisted of many dishes, which bore little connection with each other apart from all seeming to be touched with "gold leaf" or perhaps "gold paint" or "perhaps it was just glitter". In any event, this gold substance made the food inedible to him, although it greatly enhanced its appearance. In another place, he found he had made the food all wet and had contrived some kind of mincing apparatus that reduced it to a kind of pulp. This would have made it perfectly edible. In fact he was no longer hungry.*

The golden quality, which might have been real gold, seems to reflect his perception of the analytic interpretations. However, I think he pretty quickly convinces himself that I am just using glitter to impress him, and this makes the analytic food unacceptable to him. It is inedible. He can reduce it to an edible—that is, non-enviable—form using, I think, primitive mechanisms, such as wetting and soiling. However, having so reduced and denigrated it, he feels no need of it.

I would like to conclude this chapter on the deadly aspects of the personality that manifest themselves in eating disorders by referring to some recent work by Ronald Britton (1998, 2003). Britton writes about a xenocidal impulse as an aspect of human nature, much more pronounced in some individuals than others, which is characterized by an antipathy to all things that are not-self, which emanate from another. Like Segal, quoted at the start of this chapter, Britton sees the wish to annihilate need and the possibility of meeting that need as an ever-present possibility inherent in human relationships. He movingly describes the ways in which if things go well in human development, the love of the parents and the love for the parents mostly mitigates and compensates for this impulse. For Britton, envy occurs when there is a degree of xenocide, combined with a high level of covetousness. That is, when the individual has a strong urge to acquire the good aspects and qualities perceived in others and, at the same time, a hatred of all that exists outside himself (Britton, 2003, p. 126).

I find this idea of a hatred of all things that are not the self to be an extremely useful one in understanding the most serious eating disorders. I think it links up with Fenichel's observations from the 1940s that I mentioned in chapter 2. He distinguishes between eating disorders that may represent a simple hysterical symptom and those that are the outward sign of a pervasive disturbance in the whole personality and relation to reality. I think Britton's idea of xenocide, which, if sufficiently strong, interferes with the individual's entire development, may be an important factor in what Fenichel observed.

Returning now to Bion's notion of –K and the horrifying image of a relationship based on mutual and deliberate misunderstanding: Bion suggests that this situation is based on envy, and I think Britton's understanding of envy as a compound of covetousness and xenocide is a very helpful one. Patient M's xenocidal impulse is evident in her antipathy towards the other patients as well as towards the staff. They resort to force-feeding her because she cannot bear to take in anything that is "other", which does not emanate from herself. One of the tremendous difficulties in treating the most serious anorexic cases is that the nursing staff can indeed seem to the patient to be operating in –K, wilfully misunderstanding, stripping away meaning from the patient's attempts to communicate her distress. This is why it is so important in in-patient settings, where a degree of coercion is inevitable, that the staff work very hard at building relationships with the patients, which involves real understanding and concern. This relationship-building work between an individual patient and a specially assigned nurse is often called "key work". This is a very apt title in my view as this work is very often the key to the patient's eventual recovery. Careful key work can sometimes (but not always) prevent the development of the terrible situation in which M and the nurses find themselves.

In this chapter, I have described the psychoanalytic idea of the death drive, posited by Freud as an innate force parallel to the libido. I think it an extremely helpful idea to keep in mind when thinking about patients with eating disorders, particularly the very seriously ill ones. I have suggested that while the deadly aspects of anorexia and bulimia are sometimes linked with trauma, in other patients they are the outcome of development difficulties that appear to have their origins in early infantile relationships and in which constitutional factors play a part.

CHAPTER EIGHT

Assessment

While all eating disorders need to be taken seriously, some patients do, in fact, turn out to be much more ill than others. The symptoms of anorexia nervosa are remarkably consistent from patient to patient, as are those of bulimia nervosa. Of course, the severity of the symptoms varies, but in general it is true to say that, without help, the symptoms of eating disorders will usually get worse. So the patient with moderately severe symptoms now may, without help, very well have very severe symptoms in a few months time. It can therefore be difficult to make a judgement as to the seriousness of the situation, the degree of risk, and the likely prognosis. The clinician needs as much knowledge and understanding as possible in order to carry out a full assessment—hence my reason for including this chapter towards the end of the book.

Body mass index

Body mass index is a kind of shorthand way of expressing how seriously underweight, and thus how physically vulnerable, a patient with anorexia nervosa is likely to be. BMI is a person's weight (in kilograms) divided by his or her height (in metres) squared. A normal or average BMI is around 20, with 15 considered seriously underweight, 25–30 overweight, and 30+ obese. While such a calculation is a useful aid to diagnosis and prognosis, it cannot replace the judgement of a skilled and experienced clinician. The BMI tells us something about the state of the patient's body, but it does not tell us anything at all about her mind. As we shall see, these two are related, but not necessarily in a direct way. For example, a patient without a dramatically low BMI may nonetheless present psychologically in a way that is very worrying and suggests that urgent treatment is required. Anorexic patients can be at their most psychologically vulnerable when they begin to put on weight. Although they may be less at risk of complications from starvation, the beginnings of weight gain can often herald the beginnings of serious depression and sometimes accompanying self-harm.

Some specialist authorities do not advocate attempting to assess the seriousness of the illness in each individual patient with an eating disorder. Instead, they suggest trying a relatively straightforward short-term outpatient intervention, such as cognitive behaviour therapy. If this does not produce improvement, a more complex treatment is recommended. This approach continues, finally culminating in inpatient treatment if nothing else produces improvement. While this approach could appear logical, I think there are compelling reasons for making a careful and thorough assessment of each individual patient before deciding upon a treatment plan. Of course, treatment plans are always under review and can and should be re-evaluated in the light of the patient's response.

Here are some of the reasons I think it imperative to assess each patient as fully and carefully as possible.

A young person presenting with an eating disorder needs to be seen both individually and with her family, with the least possible delay. A small but significant number of patients presenting with an eating disorder have suffered or are suffering abuse and/or neglect. I have discussed this more fully in chapter 3. Before any attempt is made to offer help with the symptoms, it is vitally important that these matters concerning the protection of the young people are not overlooked. Eating disorders really can represent a cry for help.

Some years ago I was asked to see a young teenage girl. Her worried mother was convinced that she was anorexic. When I saw the patient, it was clear that she was depressed and had been losing weight. However, it was also clear that she was very deaf. It transpired that she had been born with only 20% of normal hearing. Although she had been given hearing aids, it seemed that her single mother had never come to terms with having had a severely disabled child. The girl herself was confused and withdrawn, desperately in need of help with growing up with a disability, but unable to turn to her mother for help. Both mother and daughter needed and responded well to help, and the concerns about weight and food intake soon lost their hold. To have attempted to treat symptoms of a possible eating disorder outside the context of the patient's life and relationships would clearly have been a disastrous and costly mistake.

Another significant minority of patients have suffered a trauma, or have been part of a traumatized family or group. Sometimes the traumas involve the death of important family members, sometimes the trauma may be transgenerational (for some examples, see chapter 7). We know from our clinical experience that patients whose symptoms are linked to traumatic events have a much better chance of recovering from their illness, but *only* if the trauma is recognized and addressed, and not at all if it is overlooked. A careful assessment can point to the likely occurrence of trauma in the patient's history.

I am now proposing to think in some detail about the assessment process. Much of what I will say may seem terribly obvious, and yet I think it is worth stating. I know from experience that patients often reach the stage of hospital admission and discharge without an adequate assessment ever being recorded.

One of the important keys to a good and helpful assessment is the taking of a careful history. The patient may be in no mood to give a personal history at the point of referral, and the family also may feel desperate and that all this talking and answering questions is just a waste of time. Our experience over many years of looking at cases over time suggests that if the history is not taken properly at the time of referral, it will probably not be substantially added to later on. This leaves generations of clinicians asking themselves questions that might have been at least partially answered when the case was first referred.

A detailed personal history involves not just asking the patient and her family questions of fact—although these are important too—but also trying to understand something of the quality of relationships within the family. So, for example, a mother may report, when asked at assessment, that her now teenage daughter had serious feeding difficulties as an infant. The assessor would not want just the facts, but would also want to know what effect this had upon the mother and the developing relationship. Whom did mother turn to for support? Was father involved? Or was this perhaps the start of a difficulty in the mother–daughter relationship which was always a rather secret and hidden area?

If patients and families are reluctant to think with the clinician about the past, the assessor should be prepared to justify his or her methods. If this were a physical illness, a full physical history would be needed in order to make a diagnosis. In this case the problem is a psychological and emotional one, and so a full psychological history is essential. It is helpful for parents and patients to understand that although a diagnosis of anorexia or bulimia nervosa may already be likely, that does not in itself tell the clinical team very much—not enough, in fact, to decide upon the best courses of action. It might be helpful for the family to be told that something seems to be getting in the way of the development of the patient and that this is why she has produced these alarming symptoms. The patient herself and her family might be in the very best position to help with the thinking about what has gone, or is going wrong.

As will be evident, the purpose of assessment is not simply to gather information. It is the beginning of a dialogue with the patient and, if it is a young patient, with the family too. While we are not expecting the patient or her family to the have "the answers", it is nonetheless an opportunity to invite them to think about the situation in which they find themselves.

As well as relying on what the patient and family can contribute, the assessor also has the opportunity to use his or her own capacities for observation. It is very important to be aware of the quality of relationship that the patient is able to make with the assessor. Is she able to make and tolerate emotional contact. Does she seem anxious, as one might expect, or more aloof and superior? Is there any sense in the course of the interview that she is looking for help with something that is too much for her, which has got out of hand? Or is her position one in which she seems quietly confident that she has all the answers? It is not unusual for a patient suffering from anorexia to agree to "seek help" in order to convince her family that she is taking their concerns seriously and, in effect, to get them off her back. Her thinking may well be that if she agrees to come along, everything can stay the same. If this is the case (and it often is, at least in part) then the challenge for the assessor is to try to genuinely interest the patient in what is going on, including her own reluctance to change.

Who should carry out the assessment?

Whoever actually sees the patient initially, either with her family or separately, experience suggests strongly that the assessment and initial treatment plan needs to be made by the team who will be treating the patient.

At the Tavistock Clinic, although the treatment that is offered may be with one individual therapist, treatment decisions are made and the work is held in the context of a multidisciplinary team. Specialist eating disorder teams, whether hospital based or within community settings, similarly comprise mental health professionals from a number of different backgrounds. Typically, these might include nurses, psychiatrists, psychologists, adult and/or child and adolescent psychotherapists, as well as dieticians and possibly art or drama therapists.

In practice, it is often a senior nurse who has the initial contact with the patient, but what we have learnt is how invaluable is the discussion that takes place in the team following the initial referral and meeting with the patient. The differing professional backgrounds of the staff mean that they bring different strengths to the assessment process. Nurses, for example, are trained to observe patients carefully; dieticians, with their scientific background, have been trained to pay careful attention to detail—and are often good at asking detailed questions.

Sometimes the assessment process begins before the patient is ever seen by the service.

Miss S, a 28-year-old who worked in the advertising industry, first became known to her local outpatient specialist service when her very concerned mother contacted one of the staff whom she knew slightly. She said that her daughter was suffering from anorexia nervosa, had been ill for almost a year, and, although she was being seen at her local general practice, was getting worse. The member of staff concerned explained that Mrs S's daughter could indeed be seen by the service and that the referral would need to come from the GP. Within a couple of weeks, a referral was received from the doctor, together with a report from a counsellor in the surgery who had seen the patient on a number of occasions. This counsellor said that although Miss S had had some difficulties, she was now improving, and he did not really think she needed a specialist referral.

At about the same time, the patient herself phoned to enquire about the progress of the referral. She was put through to the member of the team who was likely to see her in relation to the assessment. Miss S strongly voiced the opinion that she needed help and that she didn't feel she was making progress with the practice counsellor! She also expressed concern that a long-standing relationship was in jeopardy if she didn't start to tackle her problems. Another member of the team then phoned the counsellor, who reaffirmed his view that the patient wasn't seriously ill and that a referral wasn't really necessary. He furthermore said that he was planning to continue seeing the patient.

The team discussed the situation. They were a local specialist service and would not normally have accepted a referral if the local general practice did not consider it necessary. On the other hand, the GP had made the referral and the patient herself had phoned requesting this. The member of staff who had spoken to the patient felt strongly that she had asked for help and that she should be seen. She wondered whether perhaps the counsellor might be feeling somewhat possessive about the patient and reluctant to pass her on to the specialist team. In the end it was decided to write to the patient and the counsellor, with a copy to the GP, explaining that while someone was available to see Miss S to begin assessing her treatment needs, the service did need all parties to agree that a referral was necessary. After several more weeks, during which time the mother of Miss S anxiously approached the service again, a communication was finally received confirming that the counsellor, patient, and doctor had all agreed that a referral was appropriate.

When Miss S was first seen by the service, the psychotherapist did indeed find it difficult to assess how serious the situation was. Although very underweight, Miss S was not in physical danger. Although she stated that she needed help, at the same time she also smiled, talked about not wanting to make a fuss, suggested that her mother was rather overreacting. At the same time as she smiled, she often also seemed quite near to tears. She produced quite a confused response in the assessor and a very tense and uncomfortable atmosphere. She also talked about some very hurtful and undermining experiences at work and in her recent social life, and although she repeatedly said that her boyfriend and her family were lovely and terribly supportive, she left the assessor with the feeling of someone very much alone and unsupported.

As it turned out, her parents, who were divorced, were both rather possessive towards her and tended to be jealous of time spent with the other one. Although, of course, in one way it was evidence of how much they cared about her, it also made all contact with them extremely stressful.

In discussion with the rest of the team, it was suggested that perhaps the patient was more depressed than she was able to acknowledge. It sounded as though parents, counsellors, and psychotherapists had to be reassured that everything was really alright, even though the patient was well aware that it was not. It also seemed that the rivalry and possessiveness of the parents had found its way into the professional staff who were trying help the patient. It seemed that the patient, in fact, felt very guilty that she needed more help than the practice counsellor was able to give and so had rather minimized the extent of her difficulties and had emphasized how helpful he had been to her.

The assessor was impressed that in spite of her feeling that she had to minimize and play down her difficulties to avoid arousing anxiety in others, Miss S had nonetheless managed to get herself seen in the specialist service she knew she needed.

It turned out to be quite a relief for Miss S to acknowledge how bad and low she often felt, the more so as she felt she had to keep it to herself. She was also soon to discover how angry she in fact was with her parents and how their jealousy often made her feel like a small child caught up in a custody dispute, or a "tug of love", rather than an adult daughter with a life of her own. During the course of the assessment, Miss S also revealed more about the extent of her eating disorder. It transpired that she had a very rigid and punishing exercise regime, which consisted not only of sessions in the gym, but also of agonizingly long and lonely walks home from work, often resulting in her not getting home until after 8 o'clock in the evening. No one knew about this.

This was an interesting assessment for a number of reasons, but not least because it contained some seemingly contradictory indications. On the one hand, Miss S was severely depressed in spite of all her attempts to distract herself and others with her eating disorder. The fact that the depression was so near to the surface and that Miss S was able to acknowledge it as soon as it was recognized by the assessor was in many respects a hopeful sign. It indicated that Miss S retained the capacity to be in touch with her feelings in a way that many anorexics quite quickly lose. On the other hand, treating such a severely depressed patient has its own difficulties, and the risks of self-harm had to be realistically discussed and assessed, as well as being communicated to others involved in Miss S's care. The severity and the secrecy of Miss S's symptoms might have been viewed as a negative or unpromising prognostic feature—and indeed it did prove hard for her to moderate and eventually to give up her self-destructive rituals. On the other hand, Miss S kept much of what she did secret because she herself knew that it wasn't right. Part of her at least recognized and felt ashamed of her routine of self-punishment, whereas a more severely ill patient would have defended her actions and her inclinations both to herself and to others.

Miss S had become very stuck in her development. Although an adult, her relationships, especially with her parents, had a child-like quality, and this was what she at first brought to the assessment with her smiling tearfulness. But on the other hand, Miss S did not have a hatred of development. She knew she needed to change, and although it was frightening and difficult, she was actually asking for help with moving on in her life.

Finally, Miss S did have a wish to have relationships on which she could depend. She felt that her own needs had got lost and obscured by her parents' difficulties. But not far beneath the surface she was angry about this. She wanted to grow up, and she wanted grown-up relationships that she could depend upon .

In making assessments and deciding upon a course of action, we are taking a number of factors into account. One of these is the patient's physical condition, which includes consideration of whether her weight is stable or is falling. A patient at a fairly low but stable weight may well be in a position to benefit from outpatient psychotherapy, whereas a patient whose weight is continuing to fall might not. This implies that we need to monitor the patient over time, or ask someone else, like the GP, to do so.

Just as important as the patient's weight and physical health is the extent to which the patient's mind is dominated by death and by trends in the personality that are anti-developmental. As we saw in the case of Miss S, although her eating disorder was quite severe and her development was very stuck, she nonetheless had a wish for change and a capacity to use help to enable her to change.

We all find it difficult at times to accept help, and patients and families with eating disorders characteristically find it difficult to turn to someone else in times of need. The extent to which they are able to engage with the service offering help may well in itself be a prognostic indicator.

Patient P was referred by her school counsellor to the local child and adolescent mental health service (CAMHS). She was an academically gifted 13-year-old, but her obvious weight loss was causing concern, as was her increasing withdrawal and sense of isolation from her peers. Her BMI was 17. At her first assessment session she was accompanied by her mother, who was obviously and understandably extremely anxious. She described herself as being at her wit's end with her daughter, whose behaviour she found totally incomprehensible. She came across as a very forceful and strong-minded woman, and the child was speechless in her mother's presence. In her individual session with the psychotherapist, it was difficult to make contact with P. She declined to speak spontaneously and would only communicate by answering a series of questions that the therapist put to her. Out of this painful exchange there emerged a picture of a family riven by conflict. In the mind of the patient at least, the relationship between the parents was hostile and competitive. Within the extended family people were judged by their success academically and materially, and there was notable contempt for those showing signs of failing. The patient herself was generally contemptuous of her peers, although there did seem to be one or two who were envied and considered as superior. The psychotherapist felt herself immediately to have been placed in the category of "failure" and found it difficult to think about how she could be of help to the patient. At the same time, she and her colleagues were very concerned about the patient's state of mind, her withdrawal, and her lack of real contact. It was decided to offer an extended assessment, with regular sessions being offered, but without too much pressure to do more than she felt able to. It was felt that she needed the opportunity to establish a relationship that was supportive and responsive without being too demanding. Indeed, it was felt that it would be an achievement at this point to be able to get P interested in having a relationship at all.

During the assessment process, the mother often expressed her exasperation at the slowness and stupidity of the psychotherapist and her colleagues. Her comments seemed to hold a kind of threat that she might take her daughter away from this service to another, more competent (or perhaps prestigious) one. The CAMHS service in question felt this quite keenly, until a rather junior member of the team wondered why it would matter if this very difficult woman took her very ill child elsewhere, when they were, after all, swamped with referrals. This rather helpful question, naively posed, enabled the team to see that they had become caught up in the judgemental and competitive way of viewing things that seemed so unhelpfully to dominate the family's thinking. It enabled them to be more in touch with the dilemma of the patient and her mother; while they clearly were both in desperate need of help, they could not believe that anyone could help, because they did not really believe that anyone was good enough to help. Through discussion, they became more able to understand that P and her mother both felt helpless and terrified that no one would, in fact, be able to help. It is always easy to feel annoyance at the contempt with which some patients and their families view us, but it is more difficult to identify the sense of isolation and despair that such contempt engenders. In spite of the team's efforts, P was referred to a private inpatient service, where she was immediately hospitalized for re-feeding.

Differing ways of treating eating disorders, different theoretical perspectives, and even different services are often seen and sometimes see themselves as in competition. This is not helped by the obligations placed on services by government to justify the treatments they offer, to demonstrate successful outcomes, and in effect to prove that they are doing everything in the best possible way. While, of course, it is important to monitor and audit carefully the work that we do, and to maintain high professional standards, it is not helpful for services and treatment approaches to try to prove themselves right at the expense of colleagues who hold somewhat differing views. There is no one single answer to these complex problems. Furthermore, it is easy for services to get caught up in the kind of competitive world that so dominated patient P's thinking.

Assessing the life/death position

One way of thinking about the purpose of assessment in eating disorders is that one is trying to determine the extent of the hold of the death drive on the individual at that moment in time. This may sound somewhat dramatic, but it seems to me crucial to remember that the issue of eating or not eating is, from the beginning of life, a matter of life and death. The very fact that an individual develops an eating disorder is in itself evidence that there are powerful anti-life, anti-developmental forces at work in the mind and in the personality. The question we are asking at assessment is what other forces are capable of being mobilized against these anti-life trends and is the patient looking for support for the part of herself that wants to choose life? And, importantly, how can we know?

As I have suggested, we cannot assess the seriousness of the eating disorder simply by the degree to which the patient has managed to starve herself or by how frequently she vomits or takes laxatives. These details and symptoms are important, but they cannot on their own tell us very much. If, for example, the patient is older and living independently, it may be a long while before anyone notices what she is doing and tries to stop her. Eating disorders that go untreated and unchallenged tend to get worse symptomatically. What we are trying to assess is the state of mind of the patient and the strength of her anorexic or bulimic commitment.

It might be helpful here to think back to Bion, who talks about the struggle between the life and death instincts and who believes that in some conditions the outcome of the struggle is never quite decided. Bion makes a distinction between the psychotic and non-psychotic parts of the self and believes it is crucial to be able to distinguish these and thus identify the patient's potential strengths as well as vulnerabilities. He goes further and suggests that it may be possible to find ways of speaking to the less ill part of the mind about the illness itself.

I think this is what we have to try to do with the patients in the course of the assessment. The extent to which we are able to do this may help us to draw some inferences about how far deadly forces hold sway in her mind.

One of the problems is that we cannot always readily tell what is deadly and what is more on the side of life. Some examples might help. One might think that the young pre-anorexic, so talented and oriented to achievement, has her sights set on progress and development. She has her whole life ahead of her, and one could see her ambition as her determination to use it to the full. Closer scrutiny, however, suggests a different perspective. Although intellectually she seems to be making progress, her emotional development is rather stunted. She functions well scholastically, but in the manner of a much younger child. Her ambition is more to ward off envious thoughts (so vital an experience of growing up) than to really develop herself and her personality. She acquires A* grades in a greedy way, without any real sense of achievement. It is a matter of being terrible and unthinkable to do less well. Talking to women who have recovered from an anorexic episode in their teenage years, one frequently hears of a sense of being on a treadmill of seemingly never-ending work, from which they derived no satisfaction at all and in which they had no interest. They were not actually learning and developing their minds so much as providing themselves with constant reassurance that they were "doing well", better than the others. In effect, it was not so very different from counting calories and watching the ounces and then the pounds slip away. So an activity masquerading as learning and development, which would involve a life-affirming state of mind, has in fact been converted into the service of the more deadly aspects of the personality.

Here is an example of a patient in whom assessment of her frame of mind proved especially complex.

The patient, Ms K, was in her early twenties, a graduate, initially seen as a psychiatric outpatient for continuing and worrying weight loss. She had quite recently lost her father, with whom she had had a difficult relationship. She readily admitted that she had a problem with which she needed help. She seemed thoughtful and sensitive and was certainly likeable. She could talk with some ease about her difficult, though not impossible, family situation and about her dilemmas and indecisions about what direction her life should take. On the face of it she was a rather hopeful patient, with many positive facets seemingly on the side of life. And yet she continued to lose weight. Finally, it was decided that her physical health was too compromised and that she needed an admission to try to stabilize her weight and nutritional health. The patient agreed with this. During this admission, her mental state began to deteriorate rapidly. She became profoundly depressed and suicidal, as well as extremely angry with all the staff. Her previous good relationships with staff which she had had as an outpatient seemed to be forgotten. After several weeks of being in a withdrawn and wretched state, one of the very experienced and helpful nurses managed to engage her in conversation about art, which had been one of her great passions. She wanted to talk about Van Gogh, her favourite. She spoke of his vibrant colours, the sense of aliveness of his compositions. When the staff nurse reported this to the team, we were initially delighted and relieved. At last someone had succeeded in making contact with the patient, and it seemed that there was a part of herself again interested in life. On reflection, however, we had to remember that in spite of his vividly colourful and seemingly alive work, Van Gogh was himself a man who was seriously mentally ill and who killed himself. It seemed that the patient was trying to tell us about her internal situation. Like Van Gogh, she was capable of loving and appreciating life, but what constantly undermined her was this same pull towards death that she felt he must have experienced. It seemed that the more positive and loving aspects of her character effectively concealed the more destructive and psychotic part, and it was only her persistent weight loss that finally allowed us to take her situation seriously. The admission allowed the patient to stop covering up her disturbance, and we were all able to see a fuller picture. I am pleased to say that she went on to make a complete recovery and, with the help of a long period of psychotherapy, was able to integrate the more depressed and destructive aspects of her personality with her obvious strengths.

Another aspect of the assessment of a patient which can be misleading is the quality of the relationship the patient initially forms with the assessor. Often, patients with an eating disorder are reluctant to come to an assessment and show their hostility quite openly. Others, however, seem quickly to form a very positive transference, crediting their newly met therapist with all manner of helpfulness and wisdom. This may be a sign that the patient is anxious—even desperate—to find help, and this may be viewed as a positive sign that the patient is "ready" for treatment, or able to make a "therapeutic alliance". Often, however, the quality of the relationship as experienced by the patient seems markedly "thin" and insignificant. The patient certainly seems to have latched on to the therapist, but in a quite thoughtless way, as though the very existence of another person is enough to inspire love and admiration. There seems to be no real appreciation of the qualities of the other, more a kind of adhesive attachment to whomever presents themselves. It can mislead an inexperienced clinician, who may feel relieved or gratified to find a patient who seems to make such a positive relationship with him or her. In fact, what we may be seeing is the psychic remnant of the primitive adhesive attachment to the mother, which has never been reworked in the light of more mature attachments. Thus, far from being a hopeful sign, it should alert us to the likelihood that this is a patient whose personality is seriously underdeveloped and for whom an eating disorder represents a symptom of an underlying developmental failure of a pervasive sort.

In this chapter, I have sought to show that assessing the seriousness of the situation in eating disorders is neither obvious nor straightforward. In understanding the anorexic mind, it is useful to have input from a number of professional minds. The most helpful method we have developed at the Tavistock is to ask a member of the clinical workshop to present an account of the assessment interviews in as much detail as possible. During the course of a group discussion many important issues invariably emerge, and usually we can find a way forward with the patient. These will include observations of how the patient interacts with the clinician, as well as any indications we can find of unconscious aspects of what the patient is trying to convey. We listen carefully to the way she describes her objects. Are they all hopeless and unhelpful? Or is there, perhaps, someone she can value and appreciate? What we try to avoid is any sense that we already understand all this or that we have heard it all before. It is easy to jump to conclusions when in fact we *have* all heard remarkably similar symptoms many times before. But what is important is how these symptoms occur in the unique context and character of the individual and what other qualities exist along side them. In effect, we often find ourselves seeing the seeds of hope in what might seem an initially unpromising situation.

Even if we conclude that the patient at present is unlikely to be able to change, we can still think about how to keep her safe and to continue to make it clear that help is available. We know from experience that a patient who is not able to use very much help to change this year may be able to do so next year—or the year after. The patients are frequently stuck developmentally, but they do not have to remain so. Our assessments are snapshots of our patients' lives, not categorical statements about them, and as far as we are concerned, the option of development is always available.

CHAPTER NINE

Concluding thoughts and future speculations

An observation of mine—and one that is shared by colleagues—is that, over the past thirty years, the eating disorders population has slowly but dramatically changed. In general, the young people we see treated in specialist eating disorder units seem to be more disturbed, more seriously ill, and more difficult to treat than they were in the past.

Practically speaking, we see more dual-diagnosis patients, with self-harming behaviour such as cutting or drug abuse frequently going with a serious eating disorder. The nurses who work in inpatient units report more incidents of violent acting out and more cases of absconding. The cases are often ones that I would think of as forensic, with high levels of delinquent behaviour such as stealing, but also fire-setting and other forms of law breaking that involve police intervention. In terms of the severity of the eating disorder itself, my impression is that more patients today require nasogastric tube feeding. I certainly do not think that staff groups fall back on this course of action easily. I think it is an extreme measure, one that raises issues about the rights of the patient, and in my experience the staff also regard it in this way. The staff who work in specialist units are better educated and better trained than in the past, and some of them are very talented, so I do think that the patients are more difficult. It is not easy to account for this change, but it suggests to me that young people who are encountering serious difficulties are more likely today to show symptoms of an eating disorder as at least a part of the clinical picture than they might previously have done. This is a worrying development. It leads me to doubt the effectiveness of the educational initiatives that have been put in place.

My mind turns again to the juxtaposition of the glassy-eyed size-zero model (the dominant image of female embodiment), with the gluttonous food economies of the Western world. This external context surely must have an effect. As Christopher Lasch (1979) pointed out, contemporary culture is not solely about image and presentation. It is also a culture that teaches young people to value so-called independence and to despise vulnerability, treating ordinary human need as though it were pathological. This often makes it difficult for them to turn to someone when they are in trouble.

On the positive side, many more patients are successfully treated on an outpatient basis, so, happily, young people who in the past might have been admitted to hospital now avoid that experience.

While outpatient services vary across the UK, there are certainly some successful community-based projects offering very appropriate help. We may still be a long way from preventing eating disorders, but I am confident that we are getting better at treating them.

REFERENCES

Abraham, K. (1916). The first pregenital stage of the libido. In: *Selected Papers on Psychoanalysis*. London: Karnac, 1979.

Beck, A. T., Rush, A. J., Shaw, B. F., & Emery, G. (1979). *Cognitive Therapy of Depression*. New York: Guilford Press.

Bell, R. (1985). *Holy Anorexia*. Chicago: University of Chicago Press.

Bernstein, D. (1990). Female genital anxieties, conflicts and typical mastery modes. *International Journal of Psychoanalysis, 71*: 151–165.

Berrios, G., & Porter, R. (1995). *A History of Clinical Psychiatry*. London: Athlone Press.

Binswanger, L. (1944). The case of Ellen West. In: R. May, E. Angel, & H. Ellenberger (Eds.), *Existence*. New York: Basic Books, 1958.

Bion, W. R. (1956). The development of schizophrenic thought. In: *Second Thoughts*. London: Heinemann. [Reprinted London: Karnac, 1984.]

Bion, W. R. (1962). *Learning from Experience*. London: Heinemann.

Birksted-Breen, D. (1989). Working with an anorexic patient. *International Journal of Psychoanalysis, 70*: 30–40

Birksted-Breen, D. (1996). Phallus, penis and mental space. *International Journal of Psychoanalysis, 77*: 649–657.

Bowyer, C. (2007). *Around the Table*. Unpublished MA dissertation, University of East London.

Britton, R. (1989). The missing link: Parental sexuality in the Oedipus complex. In: R. Britton, M. Feldman, & E. O'Shaughnessy, *The Oedipus Complex Today*. London: Karnac.

Britton, R. (1998). *Belief and Imagination: Explorations in Psychoanalysis*. London: Routledge.

Britton, R. (2003). *Sex, Death and the Superego*. London: Karnac.

Bruch, H. (1974). *Eating Disorders: Obesity, Anorexia Nervosa and the Person Within*. London: Routledge.

Brusset, B. (1998). *Psychopathologie de l'anorexie mentale*. Paris: Dunod.

Chasseguet-Smirgel, J. (2005). *The Body as Mirror of the World*. London: Free Association Books.

Crisp, A. (1986). *Anorexia Nervosa: Let Me Be*. London: Academic Press.

Dally, P., Gomez, J., & Isaacs, A. J. (1979). *Anorexia Nervosa*. London: Heinemann.

Dana, M., & Lawrence, M. (1987). *Women's Secret Disorder*. London: Grafton.

Eisler, I., Dare, C., Szmukler, G., le Grange, D., & Dodge, E. (1997). Family and individual therapy in anorexia nervosa: A five year follow-up. *Archives of General Psychiatry, 54*: 1025–1030.

Feldman, M. (2000). Some views on the manifestation of the death instinct in clinical work. *International Journal of Psychoanalysis, 81*: 53–65.

Fenichel, O. (1943). *Psychoanalytic Theory of Neurosis*. New York: Norton.

Fonagy, P. (1999). The transgenerational transmission of holocaust trauma. *Attachment and Human Development, 1* (1): 92–114.

Freud, A. (1958). Adolescence in the psychoanalytic theory. *Psychoanalytic Study of the Child, 13*: 255–278.

Freud, S. (1909b). Analysis of a phobia in a five-year-old boy. *S.E.*, 10.

Freud, S. (1910c). *Leonardo da Vinci and a Memory of His Childhood*. *S.E.*, 11.

Freud, S. (1918b [1914]. From the history of an infantile neurosis. *S.E.*, 17.

Freud, S. (1920g). *Beyond the Pleasure Principle*. *S.E.*, 18.

Freud, S. (1923b). *The Ego and the Id*. *S.E.*, 19.

Freud, S. (1930a). *Civilization and Its Discontents*. *S.E.*, 21.

Freud, S. (1937c). Analysis terminable and interminable. *S.E.*, 23.

Glasser, M. (1979). Some aspects of the role of aggression in the perversions. In: I. Rosen (Ed.), *Sexual Deviation*. London: Oxford University Press.

Gull, W. W. (1874). Anorexia nervosa (apepsia hysterica, anorexia hysterica). *Transactions of the Clinical Society of London, 7*: 22–28.

Joseph, B. (1982). Addiction to near-death. *International Journal of Psychoanalysis, 63*: 449–456.

Kay, D. W. K. (1953). Anorexia nervosa: A study in prognosis. *Proceedings of the Royal Society of Medicine, 46: 3*.

Klein, M. (1928). Early stages of the Oedipus complex. In: *Love, Guilt and Reparation*. London: Hogarth Press, 1975.

Klein, M. (1930). The importance of symbol formation in the development of the ego. In: *Love, Guilt and Reparation*. London: Hogarth Press, 1975.

Klein, M. (1932). The effects of early anxiety situations on the sexual development of the girl. In: *The Psychoanalysis of Children*. London: Hogarth Press, 1975.

Klein, M. (1935). A contribution to the psychogenesis of manic depressive states. In: *Love, Guilt and Reparation*. London: Hogarth Press, 1975.

Klein, M. (1963). On loneliness. In: *Envy and Gratitude and Other Works*. London: Hogarth Press, 1975.

Lasch, C. (1979). *The Culture of Narcissism*. New York: W. W. Norton.

Lasegue, E. C. (1873). De l'anorexie hysterique. *Archives General de Medicine, 21*: 385–483.

Lask, B., & Bryant-Waugh, R. (Eds.) (2000). *Anorexia Nervosa and Related Eating Disorders in Childhood and Adolescence*. London: Psychology Press.

Lawrence, M. (1979). Anorexia nervosa—The control paradox. *Women's Studies International Quarterly, 2*: 93–101.

Lawrence, M. (1984). *The Anorexic Experience*. London: The Women's Press.

Lawrence, M. (2001). Loving them to death: The anorexic and her objects. *International Journal of Psychoanalysis, 82*: 43–55.

Likierman, M. (1997). On rejection: Adolescent girls and anorexia. *Journal of Child Psychotherapy, 23*: 61–80.

MacCarthy, B. (1988). Are incest victims hated? *Psychoanalytic Psychotherapy, 3*: 113–120.

Magagna, J. (2004). "I didn't want to die but I had to": The pervasive refusal syndrome. In: G. Williams, P. Williams, J. Desmarais, & K. Ravenscroft (Eds.), *Exploring Eating Disorders in Adolescents*. London: Karnac.

Micata Squitieri, L. (1999). Problems of female sexuality: The defensive functions of certain phantasies about the body. *International Journal of Psychoanalysis, 80*: 645–660.

Miller, S. (1998). Mouths and messages. *Infant Observation, 1* (3): 6–17.

Minuchin, S., Rosman, R., & Baker, L. (1978). *Psychosomatic Families*. Cambridge, MA: Harvard University Press.

Oppenheimer, R., Howells, K., Palmer, R., & Chaloner, D. (1985). Adverse sexual experience in childhood and clinical eating disorders: A preliminary description. *Journal of Psychiatric Research, 19*: 357–361.

Palmer, R., Oppenheimer, R., Dignon, A., Chaloner, D., & Howells, K. (1990). Childhood sexual experiences with adults reported by women with eating disorders: An extended series. *British Journal of Psychiatry, 156*: 699–703.

Rey, H. (1994). *Universals of Psychoanalysis in the Treatment of Psychotic and Borderline States.* London: Free Association Books.

Roberts, E. (1998). Aspects of introjection and its relationship to the feeding experience. *Infant Observation, 1* (3): 60–76.

Rosenfeld, H. (1964). On the psychopathology of narcissism: A clinical approach. *International Journal of Psychoanalysis, 45*: 332–337 [reprinted in: *Psychotic States.* London: Hogarth Press, 1965].

Rosenfeld, H. (1971). A clinical approach to the psychoanalytic theory of the life and death instincts: An investigation into the aggressive aspects of narcissism. *International Journal of Psychoanalysis, 52*: 169–178.

Russell, G., Szmukler, G., Dare, C., & Eisler, I. (1987). An evaluation of family therapy in anorexia nervosa and bulimia nervosa. *Archives of General Psychiatry, 44*: 1047–1056.

Segal, H. (1957). Notes on symbol formation. *International Journal of Psychoanalysis, 38*: 391–397.

Segal, H. (1997). *Psychoanalysis, Literature and War,* ed. J. Steiner. London: Routledge.

Selvini-Palazzoli, M. (1974). *Self Starvation.* London: Human Context Books.

Spillius, E. B. (1993). Varieties of envious experience. *International Journal of Psychoanalysis, 74*: 1199–1212.

Steiner, J. (1993). *Psychic Retreats.* London: Routledge.

Thomä, H. (1967). *Anorexia Nervosa.* New York: International Universities Press.

Waller, J., Kaufman, M., & Deutsch, F. (1940). Anorexia nervosa: A psychosomatic entity. *Psychosomatic Medicine, 11*: 3–16.

Williams, A. H. (1998). *Cruelty, Violence and Murder.* Northvale, NJ: Jason Aronson.

Williams, G. (1997a). *Internal Landscapes and Foreign Bodies.* London: Duckworth.

Williams, G. (1997b). Reflections on some dynamics of eating disorders: No-entry defences and foreign bodies. *International Journal of Psychoanalysis, 78*: 927–942.

INDEX

Printed in Great Britain
by Amazon

59479534R00093